I0012687

Art of Cyberwarfare

A Modern Adaptation of Sun Tzu's Principles for the
Digital Battlefield

Edition 2

By Joshua Moses

Copyright © 2018, Joshua Moses

In an age where battles are waged not on fields of earth and stone, but in realms of code and data, the ancient wisdom of Sun Tzu finds new life in the digital domain. Art of Cyberwarfare translates the timeless strategies of deception, adaptability, and strategic foresight into the cyber age, where firewalls replace fortresses, malware supplants siege weapons, and intelligence is gathered not by spies in the shadows, but by algorithms and exploits.

The modern battlefield is vast and unseen, a space where nations, corporations, and rogue actors clash in silent yet devastating conflicts. To command this domain, one must understand the principles of attack and defense in cyberspace, from the silent infiltration of adversarial networks to the artful crafting of misinformation and cyber deterrence.

This book follows the structure and spirit of The Art of War, adapting its wisdom for cybersecurity professionals, military strategists, and those who seek to master the digital battles of the future. With chapters on digital deception, cyber espionage, zero-day warfare, and defensive fortifications, Art of Cyberwarfare teaches that victory does not belong to those with the strongest firepower, but to those who wield intelligence, patience, and mastery over the unseen.

"Know the network, know yourself; a thousand exploits, a thousand victories."

Table of Contents

Chapter 1 Impact of CyberWarfare

War is waged in many forms. It is fought with swords, with words, with gold, and now with code. The warrior of old carried a blade and rode into battle. The warrior of today sits unseen, striking without sound, bringing ruin through mere keystrokes. Cyberwarfare is the conflict of the modern age, where nations clash not on open fields, but within invisible networks that stretch across the world.

To understand cyberwarfare, one must first grasp its nature. It is a battle without borders, a struggle fought in the shadows where an enemy may strike from anywhere and vanish without a trace. Unlike the wars of the past, where armies could be seen gathering on the horizon, cyberwarfare offers no warning. A nation may wake to find its power grids disabled, its banks emptied, its secrets laid bare for all to see. The attack has already happened, and the enemy remains unknown.

In traditional war, the strength of an army is measured in the number of its soldiers and the power of its weapons. In cyberwarfare, power is measured in knowledge. The one who knows the weaknesses of his enemy and conceals his own will be victorious. A single vulnerability in a nation's defenses, an unnoticed flaw in a line of code, is all that is needed for disaster. The wise commander does not rely on walls alone, for walls can be breached. Instead, he builds defenses that adapt, that deceive, that make an attack costly and uncertain.

Secrecy is both the weapon and the shield. The most effective cyberwarriors are those who remain unseen, planting silent traps and gathering intelligence unnoticed. It is better to weaken the enemy from within than to strike openly. If his systems are corrupted, his people deceived, his leaders misinformed, then his strength is already diminished before battle is joined. The victor is not the one who merely fights well, but the one who ensures his enemy is already beaten when the time comes to strike.

The impact of cyberwarfare is vast, for it does not merely harm soldiers but entire nations. In the past, war destroyed cities and armies. Now, it disrupts economies, breaks trust, and sows chaos among the people. A state need not invade a country if it can make that country collapse from within. If a people lose faith in their leaders, if they doubt the safety of their systems, if they turn against one another in confusion, then the war is already won.

This is the nature of cyberwarfare: unseen, relentless, and without mercy. It favors the patient, the cunning, the one who strikes where the enemy is unprepared. It is a war where victory is not measured in land gained, but in control seized, in confusion spread, in power wrested from those who believed themselves secure. The wise nation does not wait for such attacks but prepares before they come. He who understands the nature of this war, who sees the battlefield though it remains invisible, will hold power over those who do not.

Digital Conflicts Mirror Traditional Warfare Principles

War is eternal, though its form may change. The battlefield of the past was of earth and steel, where armies clashed and blood was spilled. The battlefield of today is unseen, yet no less perilous. Just as the warrior of old wielded sword and spear, the warrior of the digital age wields code and deception. Though the tools have changed, the principles of warfare remain the same. Victory still belongs to the one who understands strategy, who deceives his enemy, who strikes with precision and withdraws before retribution can follow.

The wise general knows that war is not merely the act of fighting, but the art of control. The strongest army is not the one that destroys the most, but the one that bends the enemy to its will. In the past, this was done through superior tactics, ambushes, feints, and the careful use of terrain. In the digital realm, the same principles apply. The one who controls information, who dictates the flow of data, who misleads his enemy while protecting his own secrets, will always hold the advantage.

The essence of strategy is deception. In ancient battles, a commander might disguise the true strength of his forces, leading his enemy to believe he was weak when he was strong or near when he was far. In the realm of cyberwarfare, the same tactics are employed. A nation may appear defenseless, allowing its enemies to strike, only to entrap them in a web of countermeasures. False signals may be sent, misleading the attacker into believing he has breached a system, when in truth he has only been lured into revealing himself. Those who rush blindly into attack find themselves ensnared, their efforts wasted, their own weaknesses laid bare.

The principle of terrain, so vital to the generals of the past, remains unchanged. In the days of swords and arrows, the wise commander chose battlegrounds that favored his forces, leading his enemies into narrow passes or across treacherous rivers. In the digital age, terrain exists in the form of networks, infrastructures, and systems. The one who understands this terrain, who shapes it to his advantage, will dictate the course of battle. He who builds his defenses wisely, concealing his vulnerabilities while exploiting those of his enemy, turns the very battlefield into his weapon.

Just as in traditional warfare, the speed of an attack is crucial. A slow-moving army is an army easily defeated. A cyberattack that lingers too long is one that will be countered. The most effective strikes are swift, unexpected, and decisive. The moment an opening is found, the attacker must move without hesitation, striking before defenses can be raised, before the enemy even knows the battle has begun. Once the objective is achieved, the wise warrior does not linger. He withdraws before retaliation can follow, leaving confusion in his wake.

Victory in any war is not measured solely by the number of battles won, but by the ultimate control gained. In ancient times, a war was not won merely by defeating soldiers, but by breaking the enemy's will, by turning his people against him, by making his leaders doubt themselves. So too in cyberwarfare, the goal is not always destruction, but control. A nation whose systems are infiltrated, whose communications are monitored, whose economy is subtly manipulated, is a nation already conquered, even if no battle has been seen.

In all things, the principles of war remain unchanged. The battlefield may be new, the weapons unseen, but the truths of conflict endure. He who masters strategy, who understands deception, speed, and control, will triumph. Those who fail to recognize these eternal laws will find themselves at the mercy of those who do.

Why strategy, deception, and adaptability are Key

In the realm of cyberspace, as on the battlefield, the wise commander does not rely on brute force alone. Victory does not belong to the strongest, nor to the fastest, but to the most cunning. Those who wield strategy as their weapon, deception as their shield, and adaptability as their armor shall dominate the digital landscape, while those who fail to understand these principles shall fall into ruin.

To master the cyber domain, one must first understand that direct confrontation is folly. In the physical world, an army may be met head-on and crushed, but in cyberspace, where the enemy is unseen and the battlefield ever-shifting, such an approach leads only to destruction. The wise strategist does not seek a single, decisive strike but instead crafts a plan where the enemy is defeated before they even realize they are at war. The strongest attack is one that leaves no trace, where the enemy finds themselves powerless, ensnared by their own ignorance.

Deception is the heart of cyber warfare. A system may appear impenetrable, yet the clever adversary sees the illusion for what it is. Just as a general might feign weakness to lure an opponent into an ambush, so too does the cyber warrior create false trails, misleading clues, and hidden vulnerabilities. The enemy must be made to see danger where there is none and to feel secure where peril awaits. When deception is executed with precision, the enemy will expend their strength in fruitless endeavors, leaving themselves open to a silent and decisive strike.

Yet deception alone is not enough. The battlefield of cyberspace is unlike any other; it shifts and changes with every moment. A wall built for defense today may become a trap tomorrow. A tactic that brings victory in one battle may bring ruin in the next. The one who remains rigid shall shatter like brittle glass, but the one who flows like water shall find a path to victory. To endure in the cyber domain, one must embrace adaptability, changing form as the situation demands.

When the enemy defends, attack where they do not expect. When the enemy seeks to attack, be elsewhere. If defenses are strong, undermine them from within. If the path forward is blocked, create another. There is no absolute defense, only the illusion of safety. There is no single path to victory, only the wisdom to find the way. In the digital realm, where threats emerge from the shadows and vanish into the ether, the adaptable mind triumphs while the inflexible perishes.

Thus, let it be known that strategy, deception, and adaptability are not merely tools, but the very essence of cyber warfare. The wise do not engage in battle unless they have already won. The skilled do not fight on the enemy's terms but dictate the course of war. The victorious do not announce their triumphs but leave their foes in confusion, defeated before they even understood the contest.

To wield these principles is to command the cyber domain. To ignore them is to invite destruction. In this war without end, where enemies are unseen and battles fought without sound, the path to victory is not found in strength, but in wisdom.

All war is a contest of strength, a test of knowledge, a battle of wills. It is not bound by time, nor does it end with the signing of treaties. War changes its form, flowing like water into new channels, seeking new paths to victory. The wise commander understands that cyberwarfare is not a separate struggle but an extension of traditional war, waged with weapons unseen and fought on battlefields without borders.

The sword and the spear give way to the keystroke and the algorithm, yet the principles remain unchanged. To strike where the enemy is weak, to defend where one is strong, to shape the battlefield before the battle begins—these are the truths that endure. The general who fails to grasp this transformation fights an enemy he does not see and suffers defeats he does not understand. The wise do not cling to the weapons of the past but master the tools of the present, for war adapts, and only those who evolve with it will prevail.

Just as siege engines and cavalry once turned the tide of war, so too does cyberwarfare reshape the balance of power. No fortress is unbreakable, no wall unbreachable, for the key to the gates may not be force, but deception. Where once armies marched to conquer cities, now warriors of the unseen realm infiltrate the networks that govern them. To shut the gates against the invader is no longer enough; the enemy now walks within, unseen, striking not at the body but at the mind, not at the city but at its heart.

The wise commander knows that victory in cyberwarfare is achieved before the first strike is made. Just as a general moves his forces into position before engaging in battle, so too must the cyber warrior prepare the ground before launching his attack. Control of the enemy's information is control of the enemy himself. To know his thoughts, to shape his perceptions, to blind him to his own weaknesses—this is to defeat him before he even raises his sword. The battle that is won without a fight is the greatest victory.

To cripple an army, one need not destroy its warriors; one need only sever its lines of command, cut off its supplies, blind its scouts, and deafen its ears. In this, cyberwarfare mirrors the tactics of old. A fleet that cannot navigate is already lost. A force that cannot receive orders is already defeated. A ruler who cannot trust his own advisors has already surrendered. The hand that holds the weapon is powerless if the mind behind it is confused.

Yet just as the offensive arm of cyberwarfare extends the reach of battle, so too does its defensive shield. A kingdom that fails to fortify its walls invites the invader. A ruler who does not guard his secrets exposes his weakness. The strong do not wait for the enemy to strike; they prepare before the battle begins. Just as a fortress is built with high walls and deep moats, so too must a nation guard its digital gates, train its sentinels, and weave defenses not of stone but of knowledge. Strength is not in the weapon, but in the mind that wields it. Those who understand this are unassailable.

The battlefield of cyberwarfare is endless, its reach uncontained. There are no safe lands, no distant sanctuaries, no neutral grounds. The conflict is waged in times of war and times of peace alike, for in this new age, war does not sleep. The enemy does not wait for the trumpets of battle; he strikes when least expected, hiding in shadows, eroding strength from within. To see war only in the clash of steel is to be blind to its true nature. The wise ruler watches even in times of peace, for the struggle continues unseen.

Though the form of battle has changed, its essence remains the same. The victor is he who understands the nature of war, who sees not just the weapons but the strategies, not just the attacks but the vulnerabilities, not just the battles but the grand design. The foolish prepare for the war that has passed; the wise prepare for the war that is coming. In this, the lessons of the past become the keys to the future. The path to victory is not found in the weapons of war, but in the mastery of its ever-changing form.

The Key Domains

War is not fought in a single field nor won by a single stroke. It is waged across many domains, where victory comes to those who understand the nature of their battlefield. In the war of the unseen, three great arenas determine the fate of nations: the contest for networks, the battle for the mind, and the struggle for economic dominion. He who masters these three masters war itself.

To control the network is to command the flow of power, for in the modern age, the network is the lifeblood of the state. The armies of old marched upon roads, while today's warriors move along pathways of data, striking not at walls but at systems, not at men but at machines. A nation that defends its borders yet leaves its networks exposed is as one who guards the gate but leaves the key upon the table. The wise ruler does not wait for his enemy to breach the fortress; he strengthens the locks, trains his sentinels, and ensures that even if the invader gains entry, he finds nothing but shadows.

Yet attack is the equal of defense. To shatter the enemy's network is to silence his messengers, blind his scouts, and cripple his advance. A sword may wound a soldier, but the severing of communications fells an entire army. The one who knows the ways of the network strikes where the enemy does not see, moves without form, and vanishes without trace. He who wages war in this domain fights not in the fields but in the void, where information is both weapon and shield. The fortress that stands strong today crumbles tomorrow if its lines of communication are severed, for a ruler who cannot speak to his men is already defeated.

Beyond the realm of networks lies the battle for the mind. The strongest walls are useless when the soldiers within no longer believe in their cause. The mightiest army is powerless when its will is broken. To control what men believe is to command their strength without lifting a blade. The wise general understands that perception is the battlefield, and he who shapes it rules the war before it begins. A whisper placed in the right ear is more deadly than a thousand arrows. A falsehood repeated enough times becomes indistinguishable from truth. The victor is not always he who holds the strongest position, but he who convinces the enemy he has already lost.

To plant doubt is to sow defeat. The soldier who mistrusts his leader hesitates. The citizen who fears his own nation weakens its resolve. The ruler who is unsure of his power loses it. The wise warrior spreads falsehoods as he spreads arrows, attacking not the body but the certainty of the mind. If the enemy cannot tell truth from lie, if he turns upon his own allies in suspicion, if he questions his own strength, then he has been defeated before the first battle is fought. This is the nature of psychological war: the enemy fights himself, and the victor never needs to draw his sword.

Yet war is not fought upon the battlefield alone. A nation is not upheld by its soldiers but by its wealth. Gold feeds armies, fuels weapons, and sustains the will to fight. When gold runs dry, even the strongest warrior finds his sword heavy and his feet slow. The attack upon wealth is an attack upon the foundation of strength, and the wise general knows that to bring ruin upon an enemy's economy is to strike at his very heart.

Just as a river sustains life, so too does commerce sustain a nation. Block the flow, and weakness spreads. Disrupt the trade routes, break the trust in markets, turn prosperity into uncertainty, and the enemy will find himself crumbling without a single battle. A leader who loses the confidence of his merchants soon loses his armies as well. A treasury that bleeds will soon find no coin left to wage war. He who controls the economy controls the endurance of war itself.

The foolish ruler sees war only in swords and battles. The wise ruler sees it in the silent struggles of networks, the whispered battles of the mind, and the unseen hand that moves the wealth of nations. The victory that is won without a fight is the greatest triumph, and he who masters these three domains will rule the war before the enemy knows it has begun.

The Invisible Battlefield

War is not always fought with swords, nor is victory always claimed upon the fields of battle. The greatest war is often the one unseen, where no armies clash, no blood is spilled, yet entire nations fall. The foolish general sees war only in the clash of steel and the thunder of cannon, but the wise understand that the most decisive battles are those waged in the shadows, where strength is measured not in numbers but in knowledge, and where victory is won without a single direct confrontation.

To fight in the invisible battlefield is to master the art of influence. The enemy who takes the field with drawn weapons is already at a disadvantage, for his movements are known, his forces revealed, his strategies exposed. The warrior of the unseen realm moves like the wind, felt but never grasped, striking where the enemy does not expect, and withdrawing before the counterblow can be delivered. The greatest battle is one where the enemy does not even realize he is under attack until his defenses are already crumbling.

The strong do not rely on brute force, for force is crude and costly. To break an enemy's army is difficult; to make him believe he is already defeated is effortless. The battle of perception is the battle of control. He who controls the enemy's understanding of the war dictates its outcome before the first strike is made. A kingdom that loses faith in its own strength is conquered before its walls are breached. A general who doubts his own strategy has surrendered before the first command is given.

The wise warrior does not need to fight every battle; he chooses the ground, the time, and the terms of engagement. He weakens his enemy without raising his hand, erodes his strength without meeting him in combat. He spreads doubt where there was once certainty, confusion where there was once clarity. The leader who cannot trust his own advisors is already lost. The soldier who questions his orders hesitates when action is needed. The people who fear their own rulers are divided before the enemy has even approached. This is the way of the invisible battlefield, where victory is won by those who shape the conflict before the first move is made.

He who fights without being seen understands that war is not only about destruction, but about control. To strike is one thing, but to guide the enemy's actions without his knowledge is the highest mastery. The wise warrior does not merely resist the enemy's attack; he leads the enemy into making his own mistakes. A force that moves without direction exhausts itself. A ruler who reacts instead of acts is always behind. A nation that does not realize it is under attack will never know where to defend. The most complete victory is not the destruction of the enemy, but his manipulation. To control the outcome of the war without ever engaging in battle is the pinnacle of strategy.

Just as water flows around obstacles, so too must the warrior of the invisible battlefield adapt to every situation. If the enemy is prepared, do not strike where he is strong; lead him away, make him chase shadows, allow him to exhaust himself in fruitless effort. If he is unprepared, do not waste time in open combat; strike swiftly, disrupt his plans, and leave him in disarray. He who dictates the flow of war does not need to fight every battle. He wins before the battle begins, and by the time the enemy realizes he has lost, the war is already over.

The greatest generals in history were not merely warriors; they were masters of unseen war. They knew that brute strength alone cannot guarantee victory, that true power lies in the ability to shape events without direct confrontation. The battlefield of today is no longer one of armies alone but of influence, perception, and control. He who understands this will never be caught unprepared, and he who masters it will triumph without fighting. This is the way of the invisible battlefield, where wars are won before they are even declared.

Chapter 3 The Cyber General

The art of war is not bound by the battlefield of the past, nor does victory belong solely to those who wield the sword. The modern general does not command legions of warriors in armor but leads an army of minds, watching over a battlefield of shifting codes and unseen enemies. The wise ruler knows that as war changes, so too must the warrior, and thus, the Cybersecurity General rises as the guardian of the new age.

The Cybersecurity General is not one who waits for attack, but one who foresees it. To react is to be at a disadvantage; to anticipate is to control the battlefield. He studies the movements of his enemies before they arise, recognizing weakness in his own walls before the enemy can strike. The strongest defense is not built from walls and gates but from knowledge and vigilance. The fool sees security as a shield to be lifted in times of danger; the wise general knows that security is the very foundation of power, to be maintained always, for war does not sleep, and threats do not rest.

A general who does not understand his terrain is a general already defeated. In the domain of cyberspace, the battlefield is ever-changing, a shifting landscape where strength today may be weakness tomorrow. The wise general does not rely on old fortifications; he adapts, he evolves, he moves as the battlefield demands. He knows that an unguarded opening invites destruction, and a single flaw may bring ruin upon an empire. He does not seek merely to build walls but to ensure that his enemy never finds a door through which to enter.

The Cybersecurity General does not wield his power alone. He surrounds himself with those who understand the war they fight. A warrior is only as strong as those who stand beside him. The untrained soldier is a danger to his own army, for an unguarded mind is an open gate. Therefore, the general does not command blindly; he teaches, he strengthens, he ensures that every hand that holds the shield understands its purpose. Knowledge is the armor of the digital age, and discipline is the sword. The army that is prepared will not be caught unaware, and the force that moves as one cannot be broken.

Deception is the key to victory, both in attack and in defense. The greatest enemy is the one who does not reveal his face, and the greatest fortress is the one whose gates remain unseen. The wise general does not let his enemies know his strength, nor does he allow them to see his weaknesses. He spreads false trails, hides his true defenses, and ensures that even if the enemy finds his way in, he walks into a trap. He who moves unseen cannot be struck, and he who is always one step ahead cannot be defeated.

Speed is the difference between survival and destruction. The attack that is met too late is an attack that has already succeeded. The wise general does not wait for threats to arise; he eliminates them before they take form. He watches the battlefield with keen eyes, knowing that hesitation invites disaster. The enemy that moves swiftly must be met with greater speed, and the force that attacks without warning must be countered before its blow can land. The battle is not won in the moment of struggle but in the moments before, where preparation determines who will stand and who will fall.

But victory is not only found in defense. The general who only guards his gates may keep his kingdom safe, but he will never command the field. To understand the enemy is to hold power over him, and to strike before he is ready is to ensure that he never lifts his sword. The Cybersecurity General does not fight battles he cannot win; he chooses when to engage, where to weaken, and how to make his enemy falter before the battle begins. The ruler who masters this art does not simply defend his kingdom; he ensures that no enemy ever dares to threaten it.

The greatest war is the one that is won before it begins. The Cybersecurity General understands this truth and lives by it. He does not wait for war to come to him, nor does he seek battle when battle is unnecessary. He strengthens his forces, fortifies his kingdom, and ensures that his enemy never sees an opportunity to strike. He does not fight for survival; he fights to command the battlefield itself. He who masters this way of war will never know defeat, for he will have already secured victory long before the enemy has even taken the field.

Qualities of a Skilled Cyber Strategist

The art of war is waged not only with weapons but with wisdom. The battlefield is no longer one of swords and shields but of unseen forces, where the warrior who wields knowledge is greater than the one who wields strength. The skilled cyber strategist does not fight with force alone but with understanding, shaping the conflict before the enemy even knows it has begun. He who masters the digital domain commands an army that moves without form, strikes without warning, and controls the battle without engaging in direct confrontation.

A skilled cyber strategist sees what others do not. He does not look only at the surface of battle but at the currents that move beneath it. Just as the great generals of old studied the terrain before battle, the cyber strategist studies the network before engagement. He understands that information is both weapon and shield, and he gathers intelligence as the river gathers rain, flowing steadily until his knowledge overcomes all obstacles. The enemy who moves blindly is already defeated, and the one who fails to see his own weaknesses has already lost. The strategist ensures that he is never among them.

Patience is the ally of the skilled strategist. The foolish rush into battle, eager to strike, but the wise wait for the perfect moment. He knows that a well-laid trap is worth more than a thousand reckless attacks. He moves with purpose, never revealing his strength until the enemy has already fallen. Like the hunter who waits in the tall grass, he strikes only when his prey is most vulnerable, and by the time the enemy realizes his mistake, it is already too late. He who controls time controls victory, for the battle is not won in the moment of attack but in the preparation that came before it.

Deception is the soul of strategy. The skilled cyber strategist does not show his true strength, nor does he reveal his true weaknesses. He leads his enemies into false confidence, showing them what they expect to see while hiding what they must never discover. He lets them chase shadows, wasting their strength in pursuit of illusions, while he moves unseen toward his goal. He who is unknown cannot be countered, and he who cannot be countered is never defeated. The master of deception does not merely win battles; he ensures that his enemy never even knows where to strike.

Adaptability is the mark of true mastery. The battlefield is never static, and the strategist who clings to old ways is already lost. The wise warrior flows like water, taking the shape of the moment, changing his tactics as the enemy changes his defense. He does not rely on past victories to win future wars, nor does he trust in a single method to ensure success. He studies the shifting nature of technology, understands the evolution of threats, and prepares for dangers not yet seen. The one who adapts will always remain one step ahead, while the one who resists change will find himself crushed beneath the tide of progress.

Silence is the armor of the wise. The strategist does not boast of his strength, nor does he call attention to his plans. He moves in shadows, where his enemy cannot follow, striking when least expected. The enemy who believes himself safe is the easiest to defeat, for he does not prepare for an attack he cannot see. The strategist ensures that he is always aware but never observed, always listening but never heard. Victory belongs to those who control the flow of knowledge, and the one who speaks too much hands his power to his foe.

Discipline is the foundation of all strategy. The warrior who acts on impulse is a danger to himself, but the one who moves with precision bends the battle to his will. The skilled cyber strategist does not let emotion guide his actions, nor does he strike out of anger or fear. He is steady in the face of uncertainty, unmoved by provocation, and unshaken by surprise. He understands that war is won not by the strongest hand but by the most prepared mind. The one who maintains control over himself will always hold power over his enemy.

The greatest strategist is the one who wins without fighting. He shapes the battlefield so that the enemy's defeat is inevitable before the first move is made. He controls perception, dictates the flow of information, and weakens his foe long before a direct confrontation is necessary. He does not seek mere victory but total dominance, ensuring that his enemies do not simply lose the battle—they never even see the path to victory. The war is won not with a single move but with the mastery of all moves, and the strategist who understands this truth will never taste defeat.

Knowledge of the Enemy

Victory is not claimed by the one who strikes the hardest but by the one who strikes the weakest point. To know the enemy's vulnerabilities is to wield a weapon sharper than any blade, for no fortress is impenetrable, and no defense is without flaw. The wise warrior does not attack blindly but observes, studies, and waits for the moment when a single blow will bring the entire structure down. Just as water finds the cracks in the stone and wears it away over time, so too does the strategist seek the fractures in his opponent's strength, exploiting them until resistance crumbles.

The enemy who believes himself strong is often the most vulnerable, for confidence breeds negligence, and negligence invites disaster. The wise general does not seek to break the enemy where he is prepared but where he least expects. No army marches forever without exhaustion, no ruler commands without dissent, no system is built without weakness. The strategist watches for the moment when strength turns to complacency, when order turns to disorder, when preparation turns to habit. When the enemy no longer questions his own security, that is when he is most exposed.

Yet he who seeks to know the enemy must first know himself. To see the weaknesses of others while ignoring one's own is the path to ruin. The ruler who does not guard his own gates will find them opened by another. The warrior who believes himself invincible will fall to the first unseen blade. The foundation of all victory is self-defense, for one cannot wage war if he has already been defeated from within. The wise commander strengthens his walls before they are tested, trains his soldiers before they are attacked, and seals his weaknesses before they are discovered. To know the enemy is half of the path to victory; to know oneself is the other half.

The master of war does not wait for his weaknesses to be exposed; he finds them before his enemy does. He tests his own defenses as he would test an enemy's, seeking out every flaw, probing every gap, and strengthening every weak point. He understands that the most dangerous threats are not the ones seen but the ones unseen, lurking in the spaces overlooked. Just as a warrior inspects his armor for cracks before battle, the wise strategist fortifies his position before conflict begins. He does not trust in the illusion of security but ensures that even if an enemy finds his walls, they will find them unbreakable.

To attack is easy; to defend is an art. The foolish general believes that strength alone is protection, but the wise know that the best defense is the one that adapts, evolves, and remains unseen. A wall may keep out the invader today, but if it does not change, it will be breached tomorrow. A strategy that succeeds once will fail if relied upon too long. The warrior who survives is the one who shifts like the wind, never predictable, never stagnant, never allowing his enemy to see where he is truly strong. The greatest defense is not to build walls but to ensure that no enemy ever sees where to strike.

He who masters both offense and defense controls the war. The strategist who knows the weaknesses of his enemy and the strengths of his own position dictates the terms of battle. The one who secures his own fortress before seeking to breach another will never be caught unprepared. Just as a shadow moves in silence, so too must the warrior of knowledge remain unseen, always knowing more than he reveals, always guarding more than he shows. The war is not won in the moment of attack but in the years of preparation before it. The enemy who does not see the trap is the one who falls into it, and the one who does not see his own weakness is the one who will be destroyed by it.

Information Superiority

The battle is not won in the moment of conflict but in the wisdom that precedes it. To see before others see, to know before others know, to move before others move—this is the way of the master strategist. Foresight is not a gift of the divine but the reward of those who study the flow of events, understand the rhythm of war, and anticipate the strike before it falls. He who walks blindly into battle has already lost. He who sees the battle before it begins will always stand victorious.

The wise ruler does not wait for threats to rise; he sees the storm forming long before the first winds arrive. He does not react to danger but prevents it from ever taking shape. Just as the river carves its path long before it reaches the sea, so too does the strategist shape the future before the battle is even fought. He understands that the enemy's intent is revealed not in the moment of attack but in the movements that precede it, the whispers that pass through unseen hands, the slight shifts in power that signal great change. He gathers knowledge as the farmer gathers grain, collecting each piece until a full harvest of understanding is before him.

To control information is to control the battlefield. The general who sees only what is before him is as one who walks in darkness, but the one who holds knowledge sees with the light of many suns. He who knows the enemy's plans holds his fate in his hands. The warrior who understands his enemy's movements bends them to his will. To starve an enemy of knowledge is to weaken him more than any wound. To flood him with falsehoods is to lead him into ruin by his own hand. The one who holds information wields a weapon greater than any sword, for the greatest victory is not to fight at all but to ensure that the enemy never even raises his blade.

The foolish believe that strength alone determines the outcome of war. They sharpen their weapons, build their armies, and march forward without seeing the road ahead. The wise know that the sharpest blade is useless when wielded by the blind. He who moves without understanding is already lost. The general who relies on brute force alone will find himself outmaneuvered by the one who moves with knowledge. The wise ruler does not seek to strike first; he ensures that when he does, it is with certainty, precision, and overwhelming advantage. The hand that guides the blade must see further than the one that merely swings it.

The flow of information is like the wind, shaping the course of war in ways unseen. The master of foresight does not rely on a single source but watches from many angles, listens to many voices, and pieces together the truth from a thousand whispers. He does not allow himself to be deceived by surface appearances but looks deeper, understanding that what is hidden is often more powerful than what is seen. He does not wait for confirmation when the signs are already before him. He acts with certainty because he has already understood what is to come. Just as the bird knows the change of seasons before the first frost, so too does the wise strategist recognize the shifting tide of war before the first battle is fought.

He who commands knowledge commands war. The warrior who possesses information superiority moves as the river, flowing around obstacles, striking where the enemy is weakest, and shifting course before resistance can form. The fool marches forward and meets a wall. The wise one moves before the wall is even built. The general who waits to react will always be behind. The ruler who sees first will always dictate the terms of battle. The war is won not by those who fight hardest but by those who understand the field before the first blow is struck.

The greatest victories are unseen, won through knowledge rather than force, through foresight rather than reaction. The one who shapes the battle before it begins ensures that his enemy does not even see the path to victory. He moves unseen, he knows all, and he controls the flow of war as the tides control the shore. He who masters foresight and information superiority does not fear battle, for he has already claimed victory long before his enemy even knew war had begun.

War is not won through strength alone but through the mastery of illusion. The one who controls perception commands reality, and in the digital realm, where shadows take shape and truth is malleable, deception reigns supreme. To see what is not there, to believe what is false, to act upon what is illusion—these are the traps set by the cunning strategist. The wise warrior does not merely attack; he leads his enemy into confusion, misdirection, and ruin long before the battle even begins.

In the world of shifting codes and invisible battlefields, deception is both sword and shield. He who moves unseen cannot be struck, and he who creates false paths leads his enemy into the abyss. The fool believes what is placed before him, but the wise know that the greatest lies are those mixed with truth. The master of digital deception does not rely on a single falsehood but weaves many together, ensuring that even the most cautious adversary is ensnared by what seems undeniable. The enemy who trusts his own knowledge without question has already been conquered.

The nature of deception is to shape the battlefield before the first strike is made. The strategist does not seek to fight a prepared enemy; he ensures the enemy is disoriented, unsure of what is real, and blind to the true threat. Just as a general spreads rumor of his strength to force his enemy into retreat, the digital warrior fills the enemy's mind with doubts, disguising weakness as strength and strength as weakness. The adversary who fears an illusion wastes his efforts preparing for a battle that will never come, while the true strike lands where he least expects.

A fortress is strongest when its defenders trust one another, yet deception is the wedge that turns allies into foes. To plant a single doubt is to sow the seeds of discord, and when trust is broken, the walls of even the mightiest stronghold crumble from within. The wise strategist does not always need to breach defenses; he makes the defenders open the gates themselves. The enemy who questions his own ranks, who no longer knows friend from foe, has already surrendered his power before the first assault is made.

The master of deception does not strike where the enemy is looking but where he is blind. To flood the field with noise is to mask the true signal. False trails lead to empty conclusions, while the real attack moves undetected. The warrior who controls the flow of information ensures that the enemy is always one step behind, always reacting to ghosts, always exhausting himself in pursuit of nothing. The one who shapes perception does not need to overpower his foe, for he has already bent him to his will.

In deception, patience is a weapon greater than any attack. The reckless seek immediate victory, revealing their intentions too soon, but the wise build their illusion slowly, ensuring that by the time the enemy realizes the truth, he has already lost. The strategist allows his adversary to believe he is safe, to trust in what is false, to commit to a path that leads only to defeat. When the moment of revelation comes, it is not the strategist who is unprepared, but the enemy who stands upon unstable ground.

The greatest deception is one that leaves no trace. The fool seeks credit for his victories, but the wise leave no mark upon the battlefield. When the enemy does not know he has been deceived, he will never seek to correct his mistakes. When he believes his failure was his own doing, he will never know that he was led to it. The most complete victory is not just in defeating the enemy but in ensuring that he never even sees how he was defeated.

In the digital realm, truth is a weapon, and illusion is a shield. The one who understands this wields power greater than armies, for he dictates the flow of battle without ever revealing himself. The master of deception does not simply trick his enemy; he reshapes his understanding, controls his movements, and seals his fate without lifting a blade. The war is won not with force but with perception, and he who controls deception controls the battlefield itself.

The Art of Misinformation

War is not won by force alone but by the mastery of the mind. The greatest victories are those achieved without battle, where the enemy surrenders not because he is overpowered but because he believes he has already lost. To control what the enemy knows is to control what he thinks, and to shape what he thinks is to determine how he acts. The art of misinformation and psychological manipulation is the art of bending reality itself, turning strength into weakness, doubt into certainty, and enemies into unwitting allies in their own downfall.

Misinformation is a weapon sharper than any blade. The enemy who trusts false knowledge is already defeated, for every decision he makes is built upon illusions. The wise strategist does not only deceive in moments of battle but creates an entire landscape of falsehoods, ensuring that the enemy walks a path of his own undoing. Truth and falsehood are woven together until even the keenest mind cannot distinguish one from the other. When the enemy moves, he moves in the wrong direction; when he prepares, he prepares for the wrong threat; when he strikes, he finds nothing but shadows. His army marches toward ruin, not because it is weak, but because it has been led astray by whispers planted long before the first sword was raised.

Psychological manipulation does not rely on strength but on perception. The mind is a battlefield greater than any field of war, and he who commands the thoughts of his enemy commands his fate. Fear is a weapon as potent as steel, and doubt is more corrosive than any siege. The wise warrior does not simply oppose his enemy; he turns the enemy's mind against itself. The general who suspects his own officers sees traitors where there are none. The soldier who loses faith in his cause fights without will. The people who distrust their rulers weaken the foundations of their own kingdom. To plant these seeds is to harvest victory without ever engaging in combat.

The strategist understands that the mind clings to what it believes, and he does not attempt to shatter illusions with force but to guide them with subtlety. A single falsehood placed in the right moment can undo the greatest of plans. A rumor spread carefully takes root deeper than the sharpest spear. The truth, once poisoned, is no longer useful, for even when it is revealed, it is met with skepticism. The wise warrior does not simply tell lies; he ensures that the truth itself is doubted. The one who no longer knows what to believe is defenseless against the one who shapes belief.

Victory is not only found in confusion but in certainty as well. To make an enemy overconfident is as valuable as making him afraid. He who believes he cannot lose takes risks that lead to his destruction. He who believes the battle is already won prepares for celebration instead of war. The strategist whispers of easy victories, of weak opponents, of inevitable success, all while ensuring that when the time comes, the enemy is wholly unprepared for the reality that awaits him. The greatest downfall is not in being weak but in believing oneself invincible when the ground beneath is already crumbling.

The master of misinformation and psychological manipulation does not force the enemy's hand; he lets the enemy believe that every move he makes is his own. The warrior who thinks he fights by his own will but follows a path laid by another is already defeated. The battle is not won when the enemy falls but when he stands, convinced that his steps are his own, while unknowingly marching to his own ruin. The one who shapes the enemy's mind does not need armies, for he commands the battlefield before the first soldier takes the field. This is the highest form of war, where battles are won not with swords but with thoughts, not with armies but with ideas, and not with force but with mastery over the unseen.

Honeypots

War is not only the clash of armies but the battle of perception. He who shapes the vision of his enemy controls the war before the first blow is struck. In the realm of cyberspace, where nothing is as it seems, deception is the greatest weapon. To fight in this battlefield is not to charge forward with brute force but to mislead, to conceal, and to ensnare. The one who understands the power of false appearances, who crafts illusions to shape his enemy's path, holds the key to victory. Fake identities, honeypots, and cyber decoys are the shadows that guide the unseeing opponent into ruin, the veils that hide the true intent of the strategist while leading the enemy into self-inflicted defeat.

A warrior who reveals himself too soon is already lost. The wise general does not announce his presence, nor does he allow his adversary to know his true nature. The digital battlefield rewards those who remain unseen, those who slip past defenses not through force, but through deception. A false identity is more than a mask; it is a weapon that turns the enemy's own mind against him. He who believes he knows his opponent is the easiest to mislead, for certainty is the weakness of the overconfident. The strategist does not simply hide his true self but creates many selves, ensuring that even if the enemy uncovers one, he is still caught within the web of lies. The one who trusts in appearances will find himself grasping at illusions, only to realize too late that the real danger was never where he was looking.

To lure an enemy into a trap is the greatest of victories, for it ensures his destruction by his own hand. The honeypot is a fortress that does not repel intruders but invites them in. The enemy, believing he has breached the walls, feasts upon the illusion of his success, unaware that every step he takes is guided by his opponent's will. He is allowed to move, to explore, to steal—but everything he touches is poisoned, and every action he takes binds him further in the snare. Just as the fisherman does not chase the fish but allows it to swallow the bait, the master of cyber deception does not fight his enemy head-on but lets him believe he has already won. Only when the trap is sprung does the invader realize he was never the hunter, but the prey.

Not all battles are won by striking the enemy down; some are won by ensuring the enemy never knows where to strike. The use of cyber decoys is the art of misdirection, of leading the adversary toward empty targets while the true stronghold remains hidden. A thousand false doors ensure that the real one is never found. The enemy who wastes his strength attacking illusions will have none left when the true confrontation begins. The wise general does not simply defend; he confounds. He does not merely hide; he misleads. When the adversary sees only what he is meant to see, he becomes blind to the true path, wandering in circles while the strategist moves with precision.

Victory belongs to those who dictate the battlefield, who control not only their own movements but the movements of their foe. The use of false identities, honeypots, and cyber decoys is not the way of cowards but the highest form of strategy, where war is fought with the mind rather than brute force. He who masters deception does not need to overpower his enemy, for he ensures that his enemy overpowers himself. The greatest victory is not merely to defeat the opponent but to ensure that he never even knew where the battle was truly fought. The war is won before the first attack is launched, and the enemy, blinded by his own assumptions, never even realizes he was fighting shadows.

Misdirection

War is not only a contest of strength but of perception. The one who controls what his enemy sees controls what his enemy believes, and the one who controls belief dictates the course of battle before it even begins. To disguise intent is to place a veil over the battlefield, ensuring that the enemy does not strike where he should, nor defend where he must. To misdirect is to shape the enemy's thoughts, guiding him toward ruin by his own hand. The wise general does not merely fight; he ensures that his adversary fights the wrong battle, in the wrong place, at the wrong time.

He who is predictable is already defeated. The enemy who understands your plan prepares his counter long before the strike is made. The true strategist does not reveal his path, nor does he allow his opponent to discern his goal. He moves in ways that invite false conclusions, ensuring that every observed action leads the enemy away from the truth. Just as the hunter does not chase his prey directly but drives it toward the waiting snare, the master of deception does not force his enemy's retreat but allows him to flee into his own destruction. To reveal one thing while concealing another is to dictate the enemy's response before he even knows the game is being played.

The greatest victory is won without a battle, and the surest strike is the one that is never expected. The wise general does not merely hide his strength but makes his weakness seem insurmountable. He feigns disorder to invite recklessness, shows vulnerability to lure overconfidence, and appears divided when he is most unified. The adversary who underestimates his opponent strikes blindly, believing himself the master of the battlefield when in truth he is the one being led. The war is won not when the enemy falls but when he stands convinced of his own triumph, unaware that his next step is into the abyss.

To disguise intent is to control the flow of action. The strategist does not act in haste, nor does he move without shaping the mind of his foe. Every word, every movement, every appearance is calculated, leading the enemy to conclusions that serve the greater plan. When the adversary believes an attack will come from the left, he fortifies his right, and when he sees retreat, he prepares for pursuit, never realizing that the real blow will come where he least expects. The battlefield is not won by steel alone but by the mind that guides it, and he who misdirects controls not only his own fate but the fate of his opponent.

The enemy who is made to believe he is in control has already lost control. The one who thinks he knows the truth no longer searches for it, and the general who trusts in false knowledge commands his forces into ruin. The wise warrior does not simply mislead; he ensures that the enemy is led to conclusions of his own making. A lie told by the enemy to himself is the most powerful deception of all, for what a man convinces himself to be true is the hardest belief to abandon. The strategist does not impose his will; he allows his adversary to believe he has chosen his own path, never realizing that every step was placed before him with careful design.

The battle is fought in the shadows before it is fought in the open. The one who sees clearly while his opponent stumbles in darkness is already victorious. To disguise intent is not to flee from battle but to ensure that when battle comes, it is on terms of one's own choosing. To misdirect is not to avoid conflict but to decide its outcome long before the first clash. He who masters deception does not fight on his enemy's terms; he makes his enemy fight on his own. The war is not won in the moment of engagement but in the endless preparation beforehand, and he who shapes that preparation shapes the final victory.

Victory in war is determined not only by the strength of the warrior but by his understanding of the battlefield. The wise general does not enter combat without knowing the terrain, for the land dictates the flow of battle as the river guides the course of the boat. In the age of digital war, the terrain is no longer made of mountains and valleys, nor is it shaped by the passage of men and horses. The battlefield has expanded into the realm of the unseen, where paths are forged from streams of data and strongholds are built not from stone, but from encrypted fortresses of knowledge. The one who understands this landscape wields the power to control all who move within it.

The cyber terrain is vast, without borders or natural defenses, yet it is not without shape. Just as the forests provide cover and the deserts offer exposure, so too do digital landscapes contain their own sources of strength and weakness. The wise strategist does not see the network as an empty void, but as a battlefield rich with opportunities to conceal, maneuver, and strike. He studies the pathways of data, knowing where it flows and where it is stored, for the one who controls the flow of information controls the battlefield itself. Just as a commander of old would seek the high ground to see his enemy's movements, the modern warrior seeks vantage points within the digital domain, securing knowledge before engaging in battle.

A fortress made of stone may resist an army, but a stronghold built in the digital realm is guarded not by walls, but by the strength of encryption, the discipline of its defenders, and the secrecy of its inner workings. Yet no fortress is impenetrable, and the wise warrior knows that security is only as strong as its weakest point. To navigate this terrain is to understand that no system is without flaw, no network without vulnerability. The strategist does not batter down the walls of his enemy but seeks the hidden doors, the unnoticed passages where he may pass unseen. The enemy who believes himself protected is often the most exposed, for he sees his defenses as unbreakable and does not watch for the silent intruder who walks unseen within his domain.

The digital landscape is always shifting, never the same from one moment to the next. The foolish warrior relies on outdated knowledge, thinking that the paths once traveled will remain unchanged. The wise adapt to the currents of the cyber realm, for what was secure today may be vulnerable tomorrow, and the methods of attack that once succeeded may soon be obsolete. The river that carved through the land a century ago does not flow the same way today, and so too does the digital battlefield change with every passing moment. To master this terrain is to move with it, to anticipate its shifts, and to strike before the enemy has time to understand the new shape of war.

Just as in the physical realm, the landscape of cyberspace contains hidden dangers, traps set by those who understand the value of deception. The warrior who moves without caution may find himself ensnared, thinking he has discovered an opening only to realize too late that it was prepared for his arrival. The strategist does not assume that all weaknesses are true weaknesses, nor does he believe that all paths are unguarded. He advances only when he understands what lies ahead, ensuring that every step is taken with purpose. The battlefield is not simply one of strength, but of patience, and the one who rushes forward without wisdom finds himself lost in the shifting sands of the digital war.

The master of cyber terrain does not seek to dominate the entire battlefield, for to stretch one's forces too thin is to invite defeat. He knows where to hold ground and where to allow the enemy to wander. He creates pathways that lead his adversary into dead ends, ensuring that when the attack comes, it falls upon empty space while the true battle is fought elsewhere. The general who dictates the battlefield does not merely react to his enemy's movements; he decides where the enemy may go and where he may not. He turns the terrain itself into a weapon, ensuring that no battle is fought on equal terms but always on ground of his choosing.

To control the cyber landscape is to control the future of war. The enemy who does not understand the terrain will stumble in the dark, while the one who sees the battlefield clearly will never be caught unaware. The battle is not won in the moment of attack but in the years of preparation that came before it. The one who studies the shifting nature of cyberspace, who moves with it rather than against it, will always remain ahead. The war is not fought in a single engagement but across an endless terrain, where the wise general does not simply fight to survive, but to command the battlefield itself.

Understanding the Battleground

War is fought not only with weapons but with knowledge. The wise general does not march blindly into battle but first seeks to understand the land upon which he fights. In the age of digital warfare, the battlefield is no longer composed of mountains and rivers, nor does it stretch across plains and valleys. Instead, it exists within the vast and shifting networks that bind the world together. To see these networks as mere tools is to be blind to their power, for they are not only paths of communication but the very battlegrounds upon which modern wars are waged.

A network is both a conduit and a fortress. It carries the life of a nation, sustaining its commerce, its defense, and its knowledge. Just as an army relies on supply lines, so too does every institution rely on its networks to function. The one who controls these pathways does not need to attack directly; he need only sever the connections, and his enemy will find himself crippled before the first strike is made. The general who does not protect his own networks invites his own ruin, for a kingdom cut off from itself is already defeated. The wise warrior does not seek merely to guard his own pathways but to understand those of his enemy, for the true battle is won not through strength alone but through control of the unseen threads that bind all things together.

The movement of information determines the course of war. The army that cannot communicate is an army that cannot fight. The ruler who cannot reach his advisors is a ruler who cannot command. The nation whose economy is disrupted finds itself weakened without a single soldier having crossed its borders. The wise strategist knows that the battle is not always fought on the front lines but within the hidden corridors of data, where a single breach can do more harm than a thousand warriors. The enemy who controls these corridors controls the war itself, for he may see without being seen, strike without being struck, and move without resistance.

To fight upon the networks is to fight in a realm without borders. The enemy may strike from afar, appearing where he is least expected, vanishing before retaliation can be made. The foolish warrior seeks to defend a single point, thinking that strength alone will hold back the tide. The wise general understands that networks are like rivers, flowing in many directions, carrying information where it is needed, and revealing weaknesses where they are least expected. He does not seek to block the water but to control its flow, redirecting its course to his advantage while ensuring that his own path remains hidden.

Deception is the key to victory in the war of networks. Just as an army may set false camps to mislead its foe, so too must the strategist create illusions within the digital realm. The enemy who believes he has gained access to a great secret may, in truth, be wandering through a maze of falsehoods, wasting his strength on shadows while the real treasure remains hidden. The wise warrior does not merely protect his own network but ensures that even if his enemy breaches the outer defenses, he finds nothing of value, lost in a web of confusion that leads only to his own undoing.

To control a network is to control the future. The foolish believe that battles are won with strength alone, but the wise understand that knowledge is the foundation of power. The one who commands the pathways of communication dictates the movements of his foe, shapes his perceptions, and ensures that when the final blow is struck, the enemy is already too weak to resist. The war of networks is not won through brute force but through mastery of the invisible battlefield, where those who see clearly move with precision, and those who remain blind fall before they even know they have been struck.

Chokepoints

The master of war does not seek battle on open ground but controls the paths upon which his enemy must travel. The wise general does not chase his foe across endless fields but forces him into narrow passages where his strength is useless. In the art of warfare, to control the chokepoints is to control the battle itself, for a force that cannot move freely is a force already in retreat. In the digital realm, the chokepoints are not mountain passes or city gates but the very arteries of modern civilization: the servers that store knowledge, the internet service providers that carry the lifeblood of communication, and the cloud infrastructure that holds the power of nations. He who commands these holds not only the battlefield but the war itself.

A kingdom may be vast, its armies many, its walls high, yet if it is dependent upon a single road for its survival, it stands upon fragile ground. The strategist does not need to conquer the entire kingdom; he need only sever the road, and famine will do what swords could not. The networked world is no different. The armies of information, the merchants of commerce, the voices of leaders—all pass through common gates. The one who controls these gates holds the power to allow or deny, to weaken or to strengthen, to grant passage or to bring ruin. The wise do not seek to fight against the tide but to control the narrow passages through which all must flow.

The servers that house the world's knowledge are like the storerooms of a great city. When they stand strong, prosperity flows; when they fall, chaos follows. He who infiltrates them sees all, for within them are the secrets of rulers, the movements of armies, the wealth of nations. The one who fortifies them stands as a guardian of the realm, but the one who breaches them holds the keys to the kingdom itself. The wise general does not strike at walls when the gates stand unguarded, nor does he waste his strength on battles that can be won without a fight. A single corrupted server can cripple an empire more effectively than an invading army, for knowledge lost cannot be regained, and trust broken cannot be restored.

The internet service providers are the bridges between kingdoms, the roads upon which all travelers must pass. To control them is to dictate the flow of war, for no army may march if the bridges are burned behind them. He who moves unseen along these paths may reach into the heart of his enemy's land without ever being noticed, while he who defends without vigilance may find his walls standing yet his kingdom already fallen. The warrior who understands this does not seek only to build walls but to ensure that his roads remain his own while his enemy's paths lead only to confusion and ruin. The army that cannot communicate is an army already defeated, and the nation cut off from itself is one that will crumble without a single strike.

The cloud is the great fortress of the modern age, vast yet weightless, dispersed yet centralized. It holds the power of entire empires, yet it rests upon unseen foundations. The foolish believe it to be impenetrable, but the wise know that even the strongest walls are meaningless if the foundation is weak. To control the cloud is to command the future, for within it lie the archives of rulers, the mechanisms of industry, the strength of nations. The one who infiltrates its depths does not simply steal information; he bends the course of history itself. The ruler who does not guard his fortress in the sky will one day find that it has already been taken from him.

The battlefield of the modern age is shaped not by the weapons of war but by the control of the pathways through which all must move. To strike at an army is to fight a single battle, but to control its supply lines is to dictate the entire war. The wise general does not chase his enemy through open fields but forces him to pass through gates of his choosing, where he is already waiting. The one who commands the chokepoints does not need overwhelming force, for he wields the power to determine whether his enemy may advance at all. The war is not won in the moment of conflict but in the mastery of movement, and he who controls the arteries of information controls the very heart of the battle itself.

Mapping the Digital Battlefield

The wise general does not march blindly into battle, nor does he rely on strength alone to claim victory. The master of war moves with knowledge, seeing the battlefield not as it is in the present but as it will become. In the digital realm, where conflicts are waged in silence and the enemy often remains unseen, the ability to map the battlefield before engagement is the key to dominance. Artificial intelligence is the eye that never sleeps, the strategist that never tires, the force that discerns patterns invisible to the human mind. He who wields it with mastery does not simply react to threats but anticipates them, shaping the course of war before the first strike is made.

The digital battlefield is vast, shifting, and without fixed borders. The armies of old clashed upon fields of earth and stone, but today, war is fought across endless streams of data, where attacks may come from any direction, at any time, without warning. The foolish commander sees only what is before him, waiting until the enemy has already moved. The wise one understands that artificial intelligence can scan the entire horizon at once, detecting movements long before they manifest into attacks. It does not blink, does not hesitate, does not grow weary. It reads the enemy's intent in the flow of data, in the anomalies that signal intrusion, in the slightest deviations that reveal where the next strike will land. The general who uses such vision commands the battle before it even begins.

To control the battlefield, one must first understand its shape. The terrain of cyberspace is not made of mountains or rivers, but of networks, protocols, and hidden corridors where enemies lurk. To move through it blindly is to invite disaster, for the adversary who knows the land better will always have the advantage. Artificial intelligence is the cartographer of this invisible world, mapping every connection, revealing every weak point, ensuring that no corner remains unexplored. Just as the great strategists of old studied the lay of the land before waging war, so too must the modern warrior use intelligence to illuminate the battlefield, leaving no place for his enemy to hide.

The power of artificial intelligence is not only in seeing what is there but in predicting what will come. A masterful general knows that war is not decided in the moment of combat but in the years of preparation before it. The movements of an adversary are never random; they follow patterns, habits, strategies that can be uncovered by those who know how to look. The one who studies these patterns, who learns from the past and foresees the future, wields the greatest power of all: the ability to strike before the enemy has even raised his sword. Artificial intelligence does not merely react to threats; it anticipates them, analyzing endless streams of data to discern where the next attack will arise. He who commands such foresight ensures that his defenses are in place long before the enemy arrives.

Deception is the heart of war, and he who understands his enemy's deceptions will never be caught unaware. The cunning adversary does not announce his attack but moves in shadows, disguising his presence, hiding his intent. The strategist who relies solely on human perception will always be one step behind, for the enemy's tricks are crafted to exploit weakness, to strike where vigilance has faltered. But artificial intelligence sees beyond the mask, detecting the slightest inconsistencies, exposing hidden intruders before they can do harm. It does not fall for misdirection, does not hesitate when faced with illusion. The general who wields such clarity ensures that he will never be deceived, for he moves with perfect knowledge while his enemy stumbles in the dark.

The greatest warrior does not seek battle where it is strongest, but where it is weakest. To break an army is difficult; to break its command is effortless. The wise general does not fight force with force, but intelligence with superior intelligence. Artificial intelligence is not a mere tool; it is the unseen force that shapes the war itself, allowing the strategist to dictate the terms of engagement. He who masters it does not fight battles he cannot win, for he ensures that by the time the enemy moves, he has already won.

Victory belongs to those who see further, who know more, who control the field before the first engagement. Artificial intelligence is not merely a weapon; it is the very fabric of modern warfare, the unseen general that guides its master to triumph. The war is not won through brute strength but through understanding, and he who understands the digital battlefield before his enemy has already secured victory.

War is not won by defense alone, nor is victory achieved by waiting for the enemy to strike first. The wise general understands that to control the battlefield, he must not only protect his own forces but dictate the movement of his adversary. In the realm of cyber warfare, where the enemy is unseen and the battleground is without borders, the art of the offensive is the key to dominance. To strike before being struck, to shape the course of conflict before it begins, to dismantle the enemy's power before he knows he is at war—this is the path of the master strategist.

The offensive cyber warrior does not attack blindly, nor does he reveal his intentions. He studies his enemy as the falcon watches its prey, waiting for the moment of weakness, for the pattern of movement that reveals where the strike must land. He does not fight every battle, nor does he waste his strength on targets of little consequence. Instead, he seeks the nerve centers, the vital points, the single vulnerabilities that, when exploited, cause the entire structure to collapse. The foolish adversary believes that walls of fire and layers of encryption will shield him, but the wise attacker knows that no defense is without weakness, no system without flaw. The greatest strike is not the one that breaks the door but the one that opens it from within.

To attack is not merely to destroy but to destabilize, to erode confidence, to make the enemy uncertain before the true blow is ever delivered. The master of cyber offense does not simply bring down networks; he ensures that his adversary can no longer trust his own. He turns systems against their owners, poisons data until truth is indistinguishable from falsehood, and ensures that even the weapons meant for defense become liabilities. The enemy who cannot trust his own intelligence is already blind, and the one who hesitates in fear of his own weakness is already defeated. The true strategist does not rely on brute force alone but on the slow unraveling of his opponent's will to fight.

Speed is the essence of the offensive, for the battle in cyberspace is fought in milliseconds. The one who hesitates, who waits for certainty, has already lost, for by the time the attack is recognized, it has already done its work. The wise warrior moves with swiftness, appearing where he is least expected, vanishing before the counterstrike can be made. He does not remain in one place, nor does he linger in the shadows he has already occupied. He is like the shifting wind, never grasped, never pinned down, always striking where the enemy is weakest, never where he is prepared. The attack that is seen is an attack that can be countered; the attack that is never known is the one that destroys without resistance.

Deception is the soul of offense. The warrior who charges headlong into battle is a fool, for he exposes himself before the strike is made. The master of cyber warfare ensures that his enemy looks in the wrong direction, defends against the wrong threat, and believes that the real attack is yet to come when, in truth, it has already landed. He plants false trails, he misdirects investigations, he ensures that even when his presence is detected, it leads only to dead ends and wasted efforts. The adversary who is forced to fight phantoms will exhaust himself before he even knows where the real enemy lies. A single well-placed deception is worth more than a thousand direct assaults.

The greatest victory in offensive cyber warfare is not merely the disruption of systems but the control of them. To destroy is simple; to command is supreme. The wise strategist does not seek to bring ruin alone but to bend the enemy's weapons to his own purpose. He infiltrates, he manipulates, he turns the infrastructure of his opponent into a tool against itself. The warrior who can move within the enemy's walls without detection has already won, for he dictates the battle on his own terms. The enemy who fights against his own corrupted systems fights against himself, and no battle is harder to win than the one against one's own foundations.

Victory belongs not to the strongest but to the most prepared, not to the loudest but to the most unseen. Offensive cyber strategy is not about overwhelming power but about perfect control, about striking where resistance is impossible, about ensuring that by the time the enemy understands what has happened, it is already too late. The war is won not in the moment of attack but in the years of preparation that came before it. The true warrior of the digital age does not wait for the enemy to dictate the battle; he shapes it long before the first strike is ever made.

Preemptive Strikes

The master of war does not wait for the enemy to strike first, nor does he allow his fate to be dictated by another's hand. The wise general moves before the battle begins, shaping the field, setting the course, ensuring that by the time his enemy realizes the war has started, it is already over. To strike before being struck is not an act of recklessness but one of supreme wisdom. He who sees the storm before it forms, who feels the tremor before the ground shakes, who acts before the threat is made—this is the one who commands victory before the enemy has even drawn his blade.

A fortress that waits to be besieged will surely fall, for it grants the attacker the power to choose the time, the method, and the terms of engagement. The warrior who understands the nature of war does not sit idle within his walls; he moves first, striking where his opponent is weakest, eliminating threats before they arise. To wait for an enemy's attack is to surrender the advantage. The true strategist ensures that his enemy never gains the opportunity to act. He disrupts his adversary's movements before they begin, dismantles his networks before they can be used, and weakens his resolve before he even considers war.

The greatest preemptive strike is the one that is never seen, where the enemy believes he has been defeated by his own failings rather than by the hand of another. The wise warrior does not simply attack; he maneuvers his adversary into destruction. He does not always need to destroy armies or shatter defenses; sometimes, he need only plant confusion, erode confidence, and ensure that when his opponent seeks to act, he finds himself already paralyzed. A nation whose leaders do not trust their intelligence, whose soldiers doubt their strength, whose weapons fail when they are needed most—this is a nation already conquered, long before the first battle is fought.

Speed is the heart of the preemptive strike. To hesitate is to invite disaster, for an opportunity seen but not taken is no opportunity at all. The enemy who lingers in preparation, who waits for certainty, who believes that he must react rather than act, has already been defeated by the one who moves first. The master of war does not wait for conditions to be perfect; he makes them so. He does not seek battle on his enemy's terms; he ensures that his enemy never has the chance to prepare. The army that is struck while it is still gathering, the fortress that is taken before its walls are fully built, the ruler who loses control before his power is tested—these are the victories of the one who does not wait to be attacked.

To strike first is not only to weaken the enemy but to dictate the course of war itself. The adversary who is forced into defense, who scrambles to recover from a blow he never expected, is one who no longer fights with clarity but with desperation. He reacts rather than plans, defends rather than advances, survives rather than conquers. The wise general ensures that his opponent remains in this state, never able to regain control, always struggling to recover from losses inflicted before he was ready. The battle is never fought on even ground, for the one who moves first has already shaped the terrain to his favor.

A strike that is seen is a strike that can be countered, but a strike that arrives unseen cannot be resisted. The fool believes that war begins when the first attack is launched, but the wise understand that war begins long before. The careful weakening of an enemy, the slow erosion of his ability to fight, the elimination of his resources, the destruction of his alliances—these are the battles fought in silence, long before the battlefield is ever set. By the time the war is acknowledged, it is already nearing its end. The greatest victory is not the one achieved through open conflict but the one secured before the enemy even realizes he has lost.

The warrior who masters the art of preemptive strikes does not fear battle, for he ensures that when battle comes, it is already won. He does not wait for threats to arise; he removes them before they take shape. He does not allow the enemy to dictate the terms of war; he decides them himself. The war is not fought in a single moment but in the years of preparation before it, in the wisdom to see threats before they become dangers, in the courage to act before others even recognize the need. The one who moves first controls the battle, and the one who controls the battle controls the outcome of war itself.

Cyberespionage and Intelligence

The battle is won not by the sword alone but by the mind that wields it. The master of war does not fight blindly, nor does he strike without knowledge. The general who marches into battle without understanding his enemy is already defeated, for he fights against shadows while his adversary moves with certainty. In the realm of cyberwarfare, where armies are unseen and weapons take the form of information, intelligence is the foundation upon which victory is built. To know what the enemy knows, to see what he seeks to hide, to uncover his weaknesses before he can conceal them—this is the art of cyberespionage.

The wise strategist does not wait for battle to reveal the enemy's plans; he seeks them before they can be put into action. The one who controls information dictates the flow of war, for knowledge is both shield and sword. The adversary who is unaware that he has been observed, who believes his secrets remain hidden, moves as if unopposed, exposing his vulnerabilities with every step. The warrior of intelligence does not engage in reckless combat but ensures that when the time comes to strike, he does so with absolute precision, for he already knows where the enemy is weakest.

The digital battlefield is vast, yet nothing within it is truly hidden. Every system, every communication, every movement leaves a trace, and he who knows how to read these traces sees the war before it begins. The enemy may guard his gates, strengthen his walls, and fortify his defenses, but if his plans are known, his strength becomes his weakness. The strategist who infiltrates his networks, who listens where he is not heard, who watches where he is not seen, strips his adversary of the one thing he cannot afford to lose—secrecy. The battle is not won in the clash of forces but in the silent gathering of knowledge that ensures the enemy has already lost before the first engagement.

The greatest weapon in war is not the army but the unseen eyes that guide it. The general who acts with certainty, who moves without hesitation, does so not because he is reckless but because he possesses knowledge that his adversary lacks. Cyberespionage is not simply the collection of data but the shaping of war itself, for he who possesses superior intelligence dictates the terms of engagement. The adversary who believes his networks are secure, his communications private, his plans unknown, is already at a disadvantage. The warrior of intelligence ensures that this belief persists even as he extracts every secret, ensuring that the enemy does not see his own downfall approaching until it is too late.

To gather intelligence is to wield power, but to do so undetected is to command the battlefield itself. The fool believes that brute force alone secures victory, but the wise understand that the battle is decided long before the fight begins. The infiltrator who enters unseen, who leaves no trace, who gathers knowledge without revealing his presence, is more dangerous than the mightiest army. He does not merely weaken his enemy; he ensures that his enemy moves according to his design, unknowingly walking the path set before him. The ruler who does not guard his secrets, who does not watch his own shadows, will one day find that he has no power left to wield, for his strength has already been stolen from him.

The art of intelligence is not only to know but to mislead. The warrior who uncovers secrets holds an advantage, but the one who controls the flow of information holds true dominance. To allow the enemy to believe he knows the truth while feeding him carefully crafted lies is to dictate his actions without force. He who trusts false knowledge fights battles that do not exist, defends positions that are not under threat, and wastes his strength preparing for an attack that will never come. The master of cyberespionage does not merely steal information; he reshapes the battlefield by ensuring that his enemy fights against illusions while the true war is fought elsewhere.

The war is won not in the moment of battle but in the years of preparation that precede it. The general who commands intelligence does not rush into combat, for he has already shaped the outcome. He does not need to strike in desperation, for he already knows where his victory will be secured. The enemy who moves blindly, who does not know he is being watched, who does not see his own weakness, is already conquered. The master of cyberespionage does not fight wars; he ends them before they begin. He does not react to threats; he eliminates them before they arise. The one who controls intelligence does not fear war, for he has already ensured that when war comes, it is fought entirely on his terms.

Vulnerabilities

The master of war does not strike where the enemy is strong but where he is unguarded. The wise warrior does not attack the walls that are watched but seeks the hidden paths that lead within. In the realm of cyber warfare, the most devastating blows are those that come unseen, exploiting weaknesses that were never thought to exist. The adversary who believes himself secure is the easiest to defeat, for he does not prepare for what he does not know. The strategist who wields zero-day exploits, ransomware, and supply chain attacks commands the battlefield without ever revealing his presence, ensuring that by the time his enemy recognizes the war, the battle has already been lost.

A weakness unknown is a weapon unseen. Zero-day exploits are the hidden blades of cyber warfare, striking through gaps that no defender has yet discovered. The wise attacker does not rely on brute force but on precision, finding the cracks that others overlook, exploiting vulnerabilities before they are understood. The enemy who builds strong defenses against known threats has already left himself open to the unknown. The strategist who possesses knowledge of such weaknesses holds power greater than any army, for he alone determines the moment of attack. The adversary cannot defend against what he does not perceive, and so he stands unaware, already conquered before the first blow is delivered.

To break an enemy is not always to destroy but to seize control. Ransomware is the weapon that turns a nation's own strength against itself, not through destruction, but through denial. The fortress may stand tall, the walls unbroken, yet if the gates are locked from within, the defenders are already prisoners. The wise warrior understands that war is not merely about force but about control. A system that cannot function is as good as one that has fallen, and the ruler who cannot access his own resources is no longer a ruler at all. The enemy does not need to be defeated in combat; he need only be rendered powerless, his strength chained within his own domain, his wealth held hostage by forces he cannot see. The army that cannot move, the treasury that cannot open, the leader who cannot command—all are conquered without a single traditional battle being fought.

A single point of failure can bring down an empire. Supply chain attacks strike not at the enemy directly but at the foundations upon which he stands. The wise strategist does not charge headlong into battle but removes the ground from beneath his adversary's feet. The greatest vulnerabilities are not always found within the walls of the fortress but in the hands that built them. The warrior who infiltrates the supply lines, who poisons the very tools of defense before they are ever used, ensures victory long before the enemy even understands he has been compromised. The adversary who trusts blindly in his systems, who assumes that his foundation is unshakable, is the one most easily undone. The strike that is never seen is the one that does the most damage, and the war that is fought within the enemy's own stronghold is the one that is won without resistance.

The battlefield is not where armies meet but where preparation has already dictated the outcome. The one who wields zero-day exploits ensures that his enemy's defenses are obsolete before they are tested. The one who deploys ransomware does not seek destruction but domination, ensuring that his adversary's own power becomes a tool against him. The one who corrupts the supply chain does not fight at the gates but within the very walls of the fortress itself, ensuring that the war is lost before the first alarm is ever sounded. The strategist who masters these forms of attack does not need overwhelming force; he needs only patience, knowledge, and the wisdom to strike where his enemy is weakest.

The greatest victory is not the one that is fought with armies but the one that is secured before battle is even declared. The master of war does not wait for his adversary to act but ensures that when action comes, it is already too late. The enemy who believes himself prepared, who trusts in his defenses, who assumes his systems are impenetrable, is the one who will fall first. The war is not won in the moment of attack but in the careful planning that ensures that by the time the enemy understands his own weakness, the battle is already over. He who commands these methods commands the future of war, for he does not merely fight the enemy—he ensures the enemy never has the chance to fight at all.

The warrior who waits until he is attacked has already lost. The master of war does not seek only to strike but to ensure that no strike against him will ever succeed. In the realm of cyber warfare, where enemies remain unseen and threats emerge without warning, defense is not a passive act but an art of absolute vigilance. He who fortifies his walls but neglects his gates is as one who carries a shield yet leaves his back exposed. The wise strategist does not build defenses that merely resist; he builds defenses that deceive, mislead, adapt, and absorb the attacks of his adversary until the enemy is left vulnerable and exhausted.

To defend is to control the battlefield, shaping the engagement before it begins. The fortress that merely stands against siege will eventually fall, but the fortress that shifts, that transforms with each attack, that offers no single point of weakness, will never be breached. The cyber warrior does not rely on a single wall but constructs layers upon layers of deception, barriers that appear firm yet yield at the right moment, drawing the enemy into dead ends and endless traps. The attacker who believes he has succeeded finds himself ensnared, and the one who moves forward blindly is soon lost. To be unbreakable is not merely to resist but to ensure that no attack can find its mark.

A castle built of stone may crumble in time, but a fortress made of shadows, where no door is truly open and no path is truly clear, cannot be taken. The wise defender does not reveal his true strength, for knowledge given to the enemy is a weapon handed to the foe. He ensures that even if his walls are tested, what lies behind them remains unknown. The adversary who cannot see his target does not know where to strike, and the attacker who strikes in darkness is more likely to wound himself than his opponent. The battlefield belongs not to the one who fights hardest but to the one who understands it best. The digital war is won by those who move unseen, who change with the tide, who never allow their opponent to find stable ground.

The greatest defense is one that is never needed. The strategist who allows his enemy to exhaust himself against false targets preserves his own strength while his adversary weakens. A system that appears vulnerable yet absorbs all attacks is a trap as deadly as any weapon. The wise cyber defender does not merely block intrusions but redirects them, allowing his enemy to fight against illusions, to battle against defenses that were designed to be attacked, while the true heart of his system remains untouched. The warrior who tricks his adversary into believing he has won ensures that by the time the enemy realizes his mistake, it is too late to recover.

Defense is not merely preparation for war; it is the shaping of war itself. The ruler who knows his own vulnerabilities will never be surprised. He who strengthens his defenses not out of fear but out of wisdom ensures that his adversary never even considers attack. The warrior who builds his strategy upon deception and adaptability ensures that no enemy can ever strike with certainty. He does not react to war; he dictates its terms. The wise general does not fear his enemy's strength, for he knows that his own defense is crafted so that no strength can break it. He does not wait for battle, for he has already shaped the battlefield to ensure that any engagement is one his enemy cannot win.

The war is not won in the clash of forces but in the moments before battle is even declared. The master of defensive cyber strategy does not wait for threats to come; he eliminates them before they arise. He does not build defenses that stand still; he builds defenses that evolve, that deceive, that shift so that no enemy can ever find their true nature. The warrior who understands this does not merely survive attacks—he ensures that no attack can ever succeed. Victory is not merely in holding ground but in shaping the very nature of war so that his adversary, no matter how skilled, will always find himself defeated before the first strike is even made.

Fortifying Digital Perimeters

The wise general does not wait for the enemy to arrive at his gates before preparing his defenses. He does not rely on walls alone but ensures that every approach is guarded, every weakness sealed, every path that might be taken by an adversary made impassable. In the digital battlefield, where threats move unseen and attacks come without warning, fortifying one's perimeter is not a single act but a continuous discipline. Firewalls, encryption, and intrusion detection form the bastions of the modern fortress, ensuring that even the most determined enemy finds himself repelled, deceived, and exposed before he can strike.

A warrior does not defend with brute force alone but with knowledge, anticipating the movements of his adversary before they are made. A fortress that cannot adapt to new methods of attack is a ruin waiting to fall. Firewalls are the first wall of defense, the gatekeepers that determine what may enter and what must be denied. The wise defender does not construct a single gate and trust it forever; he strengthens it, reinforces it, and ensures that no door stands open where it should be shut. The attacker who seeks to breach the perimeter finds not an open passage but an ever-changing maze, where each attempt to force entry only reveals his own position. The one who moves with knowledge does not fear attack, for he has already ensured that the enemy will never find a way through.

To guard the gates is not enough, for the most dangerous threats come not from the outside but from within. The walls may stand tall, the towers strong, yet if the messages passing between them are not protected, the enemy need not break through—he need only listen. Encryption is the unseen armor of the digital warrior, ensuring that even if an adversary gains access, he finds nothing but indecipherable noise. The strategist does not merely hide his secrets; he ensures that even if they are stolen, they remain beyond the enemy's reach. The foolish ruler trusts in secrecy alone, believing that if he hides well enough, his messages will remain safe. The wise warrior knows that secrecy is only half the battle, for what is found must still be made useless to those who were never meant to see it.

A fortress must not only repel attacks but also know when it is under siege. The enemy who moves undetected is the most dangerous, for the battle may already be lost before the defenders even realize war has begun. Intrusion detection is the unseen sentinel, the silent guardian that watches every shadow, ensuring that no movement goes unnoticed. The wise general does not wait for the walls to be breached before taking action; he watches, he listens, he ensures that every attempt to enter his domain is met with swift response. He does not merely react to threats—he anticipates them, ensuring that by the time an adversary is detected, he has already been neutralized.

A fortress that cannot change is a fortress that will fall. The foolish believe that a single wall will hold against all enemies, that a single method of defense will last forever. The wise know that war is an ever-changing art, and that what is secure today may be vulnerable tomorrow. He who fortifies his digital perimeter does not set his defenses and leave them unguarded; he adapts, he reinforces, he strengthens what must be strengthened and replaces what must be replaced. The enemy who expects weakness finds only renewed strength, and the attacker who believes he has found a flaw is met with a barrier stronger than before.

The greatest defense is the one that is never tested, for the enemy who sees an impenetrable wall will seek another target. The wise warrior does not wait for attack but ensures that no attack is ever attempted. Firewalls that cannot be bypassed, encryption that cannot be broken, intrusion detection that cannot be deceived—these are not merely tools but the foundations of a fortress that stands not just for a day, but for all time. The war is not won in battle alone but in the quiet moments before it, where the one who prepares most thoroughly ensures that he never needs to fight at all.

Redundancy and Resilience

The wise general does not place all his forces in a single stronghold, nor does he rely on a single path to victory. He who builds his kingdom upon a single foundation invites ruin, for when that foundation crumbles, all is lost. The master of war understands that true strength lies not in unyielding walls but in the ability to endure, to adapt, and to rise again even when struck. The essence of resilience is not merely to withstand attack but to ensure that no single strike, no single failure, can bring total defeat. In the realm of digital warfare, where no system is impenetrable and no defense is absolute, redundancy is the safeguard that ensures survival, and resilience is the force that turns weakness into strength.

A fortress with only one gate is a prison to its own defenders. If that gate is taken, there is no escape, and the kingdom within is doomed. The wise ruler does not trust a single point of entry, nor does he rely on a single means of protection. He builds hidden paths, secret routes, and fallback positions so that even if one defense is breached, another stands in its place. A system that depends on a single line of defense is already vulnerable, for the enemy need only strike once to claim victory. The strategist ensures that his networks, his resources, and his lines of communication are layered, so that even if one is cut, another remains. To have redundancy is not to prepare for failure but to guarantee that failure never brings collapse.

A tree that bends in the storm does not break, while the rigid branch snaps under the weight of the wind. The warrior who trusts in the illusion of invincibility is the one most easily destroyed, for he does not prepare for the moment when his strength is tested. The master of war does not build a system that cannot be breached; he builds one that can recover when it is. He does not seek only to prevent disaster but to ensure that when disaster comes, it does not bring ruin. A single failure must never lead to total defeat. The wise ensure that even in times of great loss, there remains a path to regain what has been taken.

The river that is blocked does not cease to flow; it finds a new path. The strategist understands that no defense is eternal, no system unbreakable, and no fortress beyond the reach of time. The true art of war is not to stand unmoved but to move with the tide, adapting, evolving, and ensuring that no adversary can strike a fatal blow. The enemy who believes he has succeeded in bringing ruin must find himself mistaken when the defenses shift, the systems restore, and what was lost is rebuilt stronger than before. The attack that does not bring final victory is no attack at all, for he who rises again is never truly defeated.

A kingdom that does not prepare for loss invites destruction. The ruler who believes he will never be struck does not prepare for the moment he is. The general who assumes his walls will never fall does not plan for the day they crumble. The wise understand that redundancy is not excess, but necessity; that resilience is not weakness, but the highest form of strength. To endure is to control the battlefield, for the war is not decided by a single battle but by the force that remains standing when all else has fallen. The one who prepares for recovery as much as for defense ensures that no strike, no loss, no disaster will ever bring an end to his dominion. He who masters resilience does not fear attack, for he has already ensured that no enemy will ever see him truly fall.

Incident Response

The warrior who waits until the enemy has overrun his walls has already lost the battle. The master of war does not react in panic but moves with precision, ensuring that every threat is met with swift and decisive action. In the realm of cyber warfare, where the enemy strikes without warning and vanishes before he is seen, the ability to respond without hesitation is the difference between survival and destruction. To master incident response is to control the battle before it spreads, to recognize danger before it grows, and to ensure that the enemy's strike is turned against him before it can achieve its purpose.

The wise strategist does not wait for the full force of an attack before acting. He understands that by the time the battle is visible, it may already be lost. The first sign of intrusion is not a moment for deliberation but for immediate execution of a well-rehearsed plan. The adversary who believes his movements are undetected must find himself ensnared before he can cause damage. The one who hesitates, who delays, who doubts, gives his enemy the space to expand, to dig deeper, to turn a minor breach into a catastrophic failure. The warrior of the digital battlefield does not allow such an advantage to his foe; he moves with speed, sealing off the path of attack before the invader can claim more ground.

To contain an enemy is to deny him freedom, to remove his ability to maneuver, to force him into a position where he can do no harm. Just as a fire must be deprived of air to be extinguished, so too must a cyber threat be deprived of access, of control, of any means to spread further. The attacker who is met with swift containment does not find victory but finds himself trapped within a space that offers him no escape. The general who understands this ensures that his response is not chaotic but precise, cutting off the enemy's options one by one, leaving him isolated and powerless. The adversary who is encircled and unable to advance is already defeated, for he has nothing left to exploit.

A battle is not won by defense alone, but by the ability to take control of the field once again. To remove an intruder is not enough; the breach must be sealed, the weaknesses fortified, and the lessons learned. The wise warrior does not simply repair the damage but ensures that the same strike can never be used against him again. The enemy who returns to find his former path of attack blocked is an enemy who is already at a disadvantage. The leader who restores his forces while strengthening his defenses does not merely survive an attack but emerges stronger from it. The battle is not decided by whether one is struck but by whether one can rise again with greater strength.

The greatest warrior does not fear an attack, for he has already prepared for it. The one who commands incident response does not react with uncertainty but with the clarity of one who has fought this battle many times before it ever occurred. His plans are not written in the moment of crisis but have been crafted long before, tested and refined until they are as precise as the strike of a blade. The adversary who seeks to cause destruction finds not a helpless target but an enemy ready to meet him at every step. The war is not won in the absence of threats, but in the mastery of response, in the ability to turn any attack into a failure for the one who launched it. The warrior who understands this truth stands unshaken, for no enemy, no breach, no attack will ever find him unprepared.

The warrior who stands alone, no matter how skilled, will one day find himself overwhelmed. The master of war does not seek victory through strength alone but through the wisdom of alliances, for he understands that the greatest battles are not fought by a single force but by many moving as one. In the realm of cyberwarfare, where threats emerge without warning and enemies strike from the shadows, the power of a single nation, a single system, or a single defender is never enough. To form alliances is to weave a shield that no adversary can break, to create a network of strength that extends beyond the reach of any one force. The wise strategist does not wait until he is under siege to seek allies but builds his foundation before war ever begins, ensuring that when conflict comes, he does not face it alone.

A kingdom that fortifies its own walls yet ignores those of its neighbors is a kingdom that will one day fall. The enemy does not always attack the strongest target but seeks the weakest point, and if that weakness lies beyond one's own domain, it is still a path to ruin. The general who understands the nature of war does not merely strengthen his own defenses but ensures that those who stand beside him are equally fortified. An ally's fall is an opening for the enemy, and to allow weakness in one's circle is to invite destruction upon oneself. The strategist who cultivates strong alliances ensures that no weakness exists within his ranks, that no breach in a distant wall becomes the path through which the enemy gains entry.

To stand united is not only to share strength but to multiply intelligence. The master of cyberwarfare knows that knowledge is the greatest weapon and that he who controls information controls the battlefield. No single warrior can see all, but a network of many eyes ensures that no threat goes unnoticed. To form alliances is to extend one's vision, to gather intelligence from many sources, to anticipate attacks before they are launched. The enemy who believes he moves unseen will find himself revealed, for his actions are watched from all sides. The strategist who commands such a network ensures that his forces are never caught unaware, for where one ally may not see, another will, and together they will move with the wisdom of a force greater than any single mind.

A single sword may be broken, but an army moves as an unyielding force. The adversary who seeks to isolate his target will find himself facing not one opponent but many, striking from all directions, responding with coordinated strength. The wise general does not rely only on his own power but ensures that in times of attack, he can call upon forces beyond his own command. The enemy who strikes at one will find himself striking at all, and the war that he sought to wage against a single opponent will become a conflict that he cannot hope to win. The alliances that are forged in times of peace are the weapons that ensure victory in war, and the warrior who neglects them will find himself alone when the battle is at its fiercest.

The greatest alliance is not only one of strength but one of trust. The strategist who forms alliances based on convenience alone will one day find that they crumble when most needed. The true master of war cultivates bonds that endure, ensuring that those who stand beside him do so not out of necessity but out of shared purpose. The warrior who trusts his allies as he trusts his own hand moves with confidence, knowing that when the moment of battle comes, he does not fight alone. The enemy who faces such a force does not face scattered resistance but a unified strength that no single attack can break.

Victory in cyberwarfare is not claimed by the strongest, nor is it guaranteed to the most cunning. It belongs to those who understand that war is not won in isolation but through the mastery of alliances, through the weaving of a force greater than any single entity. The one who stands alone will fall alone, but the one who moves as part of a greater force will find that no enemy, no attack, no threat can overcome him. The war is not fought by one but by many, and he who commands the loyalty, trust, and strength of his allies has already secured his place on the battlefield before the first strike is ever made.

Collective Cybersecurity

The wise general knows that war is not fought alone. A single fortress, no matter how strong, will one day fall if it stands isolated, for the enemy who cannot breach the walls directly will instead encircle it, cutting off its lifeblood until it crumbles from within. The master of strategy understands that strength is not merely in one's own defenses but in the power of those who stand beside him. In the realm of cyberwarfare, where enemies move unseen and strike without warning, the power of collective security is the force that turns vulnerability into invincibility. He who joins with others in defense ensures that no adversary can break him, for his strength is multiplied beyond the reach of any single foe.

A nation that guards only its own gates invites attack, for the enemy need only strike where no sentinel stands. The foolish ruler believes that his own walls are enough, that his defenses will hold while others fall. The wise ruler sees that the battlefield is larger than his own domain, that to fight alone is to fight blind, and that a shared defense is the only true defense. Alliances such as NATO and Five Eyes are not merely agreements of cooperation; they are shields forged by many hands, each reinforcing the other, each ensuring that no weakness is left exposed.

The enemy who might strike at one must contend with all, and the war that he believed could be won in isolation becomes a battle against an unbreakable force.

To see beyond one's own borders is to command the battlefield before the enemy makes his move. The lone warrior can only see what lies before him, but an alliance of many ensures that no approach goes unnoticed. The enemy who moves in darkness finds himself revealed, for where one eye may fail, many will see. Intelligence shared is strength multiplied, and the one who understands this ensures that no adversary can advance without being detected, no threat can take form without being countered. The alliances that bind nations together in cybersecurity are not merely agreements of trust; they are weapons of foresight, ensuring that by the time an enemy strikes, his every move has already been seen and understood.

A castle that stands alone will fall when its supplies are cut, but a network of fortresses ensures that no single point of failure exists. The master of war does not place his fate in a single defense but ensures that if one wall falls, another stands behind it. In cybersecurity, where threats evolve and defenses are tested with each passing day, redundancy is the key to survival. The alliances that unite nations in digital defense ensure that no weakness remains unguarded, that no enemy can find an easy path to victory. The attack that might cripple one system is absorbed by the strength of many, and the war that might be lost alone is won through collective resilience.

The enemy who seeks to divide will always fail against those who stand together. The adversary who hopes to exploit weakness finds that every gap is already covered, every path already blocked. The ruler who commands collective cybersecurity efforts ensures that no adversary can ever strike with certainty, for his power is no longer limited to his own domain. He does not fight merely with his own knowledge but with the knowledge of all who stand with him. He does not defend alone but with the strength of many shields, each reinforcing the other, each ensuring that no single breach can bring destruction.

Victory in cyberwarfare belongs not to the solitary defender but to the one who moves with an army unseen, who fights not as one but as many, who ensures that no enemy can ever isolate him. The alliances that bind nations together in cybersecurity are not merely agreements; they are the future of war itself, the force that turns vulnerability into strength, the shield that ensures that no adversary will ever find an easy victory. The war is not won by those who stand alone but by those who understand that true power lies in unity, in foresight, and in the ability to strike as one. The master of war does not merely prepare for attack; he ensures that when war comes, he does not fight it alone.

Coordinated Defense

The master of war does not fight with strength alone but with knowledge, and the greatest knowledge is that which is shared among allies. The warrior who guards only his own domain is blind to the greater battle, for the enemy does not strike one fortress at a time but seeks to exploit the gaps between them. The wise general understands that a defense that stands alone will one day fall, but a defense that moves as one, where knowledge flows freely, ensures that no adversary can advance unnoticed, no threat can spread unchecked. Coordinated defense is not merely a shield against attack; it is the very foundation of dominance, the force that ensures no weakness can ever be exploited.

A ruler who trusts only his own eyes is a ruler who sees little. The battlefield of cyberspace is vast, shifting, and filled with deception. No single warrior can watch every path, no single force can stand against the full weight of an enemy that moves unseen. The strategist who commands intelligence sharing ensures that what one defender does not see, another does. He who learns only from his own battles fights with limited knowledge, but he who draws from the wisdom of many fights with the experience of a thousand victories. The enemy who moves in secrecy finds himself revealed, for the watchful eyes of many leave no shadow unexamined. To fight with knowledge is to ensure that by the time an attack is launched, it has already been met with an unbreakable response.

Strength lies not in isolation but in coordination. The warrior who fights without communication is already defeated, for he does not know where the battle is strongest or where his allies need reinforcement. A fortress that does not warn another of approaching danger is a fortress that dooms its neighbor to ruin. The wise general does not simply defend his own walls; he ensures that every stronghold is fortified, that every warrior is informed, that every attack is met not by one but by many. The enemy who seeks to strike at a single point finds himself met with an entire force, his path blocked, his strength divided, his attack turned to failure before it has even begun.

War is not won through reaction alone but through preparation. The strategist who relies on defense alone has already surrendered control of the battlefield to his enemy. The master of war ensures that his forces do not merely guard against threats but anticipate them, moving together as a single entity, closing vulnerabilities before they can be exploited. He does not wait for an attack to come; he ensures that by the time his enemy moves, his defenses have already shifted to meet him. The adversary who expects disorder finds only discipline, and the attacker who believes he strikes in secret discovers that he has been expected all along.

A defense that does not learn is a defense that will eventually fail. The warrior who does not evolve with his enemy is one who will one day fall before him. Intelligence is not merely to be gathered but to be shared, refined, and used to shape future battles. The wise general does not fight today's war with yesterday's knowledge; he ensures that every lesson learned becomes a weapon, that every weakness found is sealed, that every tactic discovered is used against its originator. The enemy who believes he can repeat his successes finds himself facing a force that has already adapted, already strengthened, already turned his past victories into future defeats.

The greatest strength in cyberwarfare is not in a single fortress, a single defense, or a single warrior, but in the coordination of many, in the seamless sharing of knowledge, in the ability to move as one while the enemy struggles in isolation. The adversary who fights against such a force does not face a mere wall of resistance; he faces a shifting, evolving battlefield where no weakness remains open for long, where every step forward is met with forces already prepared to counter him. The war is not won through numbers alone, nor through the strength of any single defender, but through the power of those who stand together, who learn together, and who ensure that no enemy will ever find them unprepared.

Private Sector Cyber Defense

The wise general understands that war is not fought by armies alone, nor is victory secured through the strength of governments without the support of those who stand beyond the battlefield. In the realm of cyber warfare, where the lines between war and commerce blur, the private sector is not merely an observer but a crucial force in national defense. The master of strategy knows that a kingdom that relies only on its own soldiers is a kingdom that leaves its flanks exposed, for the roads upon which its armies move, the weapons with which they fight, and the intelligence upon which they act all rest in the hands of those outside its formal command. The ruler who does not forge alliances with the private sector fights with only half his strength, while the one who harnesses the full power of industry ensures that his nation stands unshaken against any foe.

The battlefield of cyberspace does not belong solely to governments, for the enemy does not strike only at military strongholds. He moves through the networks of commerce, infiltrates the corridors of finance, and seizes control of the lifeblood of a nation's economy. A kingdom that guards its military secrets but leaves its industries unprotected has already invited its own destruction. The warrior who seeks to command the digital battlefield must recognize that the greatest vulnerabilities often lie not in the arsenals of war but in the infrastructure that sustains the nation itself. The adversary who disables a military force may delay a war, but the one who cripples the flow of commerce, who disrupts the power grids, who seizes control of communication networks, ensures that the war is lost before the first battle is fought. The wise ruler does not see private companies as separate from the defense of the nation but as the very foundation upon which national security stands.

The strength of a nation's cyber defense is not measured by its weapons alone but by the knowledge it commands. The enemy does not march in the open but hides within the endless flow of information, striking with precision where the defenses are weakest. The private sector holds the keys to these pathways, for its networks carry the vast streams of data upon which a nation depends. He who commands this knowledge does not merely react to threats; he anticipates them, ensuring that no enemy may move unseen, no attack may go unnoticed, no vulnerability may remain unguarded. The general who believes he can wage war without the support of those who control these networks is a general who fights in darkness, while his enemy moves in the light. The ruler who builds strong ties with private industry ensures that he sees all, for every company, every system, every line of code becomes an extension of his own army, each watching for the first sign of intrusion, each acting as an unyielding barrier against those who seek to breach the nation's defenses.

The greatest fortresses are not built by warriors alone, nor are the most impenetrable walls raised solely by those who wield power. The private sector, with its mastery of innovation, its ability to move swiftly, its control over the very technology upon which modern war is waged, is the silent army that stands between security and chaos. The ruler who ignores this force will find himself ill-equipped for the battles of the future, for the war of today is not fought with steel but with data, not with soldiers alone but with the engineers, developers, and architects who shape the very terrain upon which cyber battles are won and lost. The wise strategist does not attempt to fight alone but forges alliances with those who understand the battlefield better than any general, ensuring that every innovation becomes a shield, every advancement a weapon, every breakthrough a step toward invincibility.

The nation that does not value its private sector in cyber defense stands upon fragile ground, for it relies upon tools it does not control, upon technologies it does not fully understand, and upon systems that are defended not by its own warriors but by those who may not yet realize they are part of the battle. The enemy who seeks to strike at such a nation does not need to breach its military defenses; he need only infiltrate the industries that sustain it, the companies that fuel its progress, the minds that drive its innovation. The master of war sees this danger before it arises and ensures that no such weakness exists. He brings the private sector into the fold, transforming every business into a sentinel, every company into a guardian, every network into an unbreakable chain of defense. He ensures that when the enemy comes, he does not face a single army but an entire nation—government and industry standing together, unshaken, unyielding, undefeatable.

Victory in cyberwarfare is not secured through strength alone but through unity, through the seamless collaboration of those who command knowledge, control technology, and wield power. The ruler who understands this does not merely defend his nation; he fortifies it beyond the reach of any adversary. The war is not fought by governments alone, nor is it won by those who rely only on their own forces. The one who builds strong alliances with the private sector, who ensures that no weakness is left exposed, who transforms every company into a pillar of security, does not fear attack—for he has already ensured that no enemy will ever find a way through.

The warrior who conquers the mind need not conquer the body. The master of war understands that true victory is not in battle alone but in the breaking of the enemy's will. In the realm of cyberspace, where armies do not march and fortresses do not stand upon the earth, the greatest weapon is not steel or fire but the ability to shape perception, to control belief, to dictate what is real and what is illusion. Psychological warfare in cyberspace is the art of bending reality itself, ensuring that by the time the enemy realizes he is at war, he has already been defeated.

A kingdom does not fall when its walls are breached; it falls when its people no longer believe in its strength. The adversary who doubts his own leaders, who mistrusts his own institutions, who fears that his cause is already lost, is one who fights not against an external foe but against himself. The wise strategist does not always need to strike directly; he plants seeds of uncertainty, whispers that turn into storms, shadows that move unseen yet cast doubt upon all that was once certain. The army that hesitates, the commander who no longer trusts his orders, the people who question their own security—these are victories won without a single battle, conquests secured without the raising of a single sword.

The enemy who controls information controls the war. The truth is a weapon, but so too is the lie, for the mind that cannot distinguish one from the other is defenseless against both. The master of psychological warfare does not simply spread deception; he ensures that truth itself becomes uncertain. The ruler who no longer knows which reports to trust, the general who questions whether his own ranks have been infiltrated, the nation that no longer knows if its allies will stand beside it—these are the defeats that ensure an empire collapses from within. The adversary who fights against ghosts, who expends his strength preparing for battles that do not exist, who turns upon his own allies in paranoia, is an adversary already conquered.

Fear is the most potent of weapons, for the enemy who fears does not act with clarity. A strike upon his mind is greater than a strike upon his walls, for walls can be rebuilt, but faith once lost is not easily regained. The wise general does not seek only to spread terror but to direct it, ensuring that the enemy sees danger where none exists, that he fortifies where no attack is coming, that he exhausts himself chasing illusions. The warrior who fights an unseen foe is one who tires long before the true enemy ever arrives. The master of cyberspace does not need to be everywhere; he need only ensure that his adversary believes he is.

A nation divided is a nation defeated. The ruler who does not command the loyalty of his people, the leader who is questioned by his own army, the society that fractures under the weight of uncertainty—these are lands that fall before the first sword is drawn. Psychological warfare is not merely the shaping of perception but the breaking of unity, the slow erosion of trust, the careful manipulation of belief until the enemy turns against himself. The greatest victory is not to destroy but to control, to ensure that the enemy no longer knows whether he fights his true opponent or his own reflection.

The war in cyberspace is not fought with weapons alone but with ideas, with fear, with deception. The one who commands these forces does not fear the strength of his enemy, for he ensures that his enemy's strength is never fully realized. The adversary who no longer knows what to trust, who no longer knows where to strike, who no longer knows if he is even winning, is already lost. The master of psychological warfare does not need to conquer nations—he ensures that they crumble by their own hands. The war is not won in the clash of armies but in the silence before it, where the mind is shaped long before the battle ever begins.

Social Engineering

To master the battlefield of the mind, one must first understand the nature of deception. War is not fought only with armies and weapons, but with whispers, with rumors, with the slow erosion of truth until what remains is a landscape shaped by the will of the cunning. Social engineering, propaganda, and the weaponization of information are the silent swords of those who seek to conquer without open battle, to enslave without shackles, to command without the vanquished even realizing they have surrendered.

The greatest victory is not in the destruction of an enemy's army but in the shaping of their thoughts before battle begins. To engineer society is to shape its desires, its fears, its loyalties. A ruler does not need to command obedience if the people themselves have been led to believe that compliance is their own will. The strategist who understands human nature understands that people crave belonging, that they are swayed by authority, that repetition builds truth in the minds of the uncertain. By manipulating these instincts, the ruler does not need to suppress rebellion—it will not arise, for the people will see no chains even when bound.

Propaganda is the art of war fought within the soul. It is not merely the distribution of lies but the careful construction of belief. A falsehood told without purpose is a wasted breath, but a falsehood woven into the fabric of truth becomes indistinguishable, a seed planted deep that will grow into conviction. He who wields propaganda does not demand loyalty; he nurtures it. He does not argue against dissent; he makes the dissenter a villain before the first word is spoken. By controlling the narrative, he does not only shape history but the very way people perceive reality itself.

The weaponization of information is the blade hidden in the cloak, the strike unseen until the wound festers. A kingdom does not fall merely when its walls are breached but when its people no longer believe in its strength. To use information as a weapon is to turn knowledge against its holder. Truth can be twisted to destroy just as easily as falsehood can be used to build. A scandal need not be true to ruin a reputation; an accusation, whispered enough times, becomes a sentence before judgment is passed. The clever general weakens his enemy not by destroying his weapons, but by making his own soldiers distrust them. A people who no longer know what to believe will believe in nothing, and a nation that believes in nothing is already lost.

To defend against these unseen forces, one must first recognize their presence. The wise do not accept every word as truth, nor do they dismiss all as lies. They see the intent behind the message, they question who benefits, they understand that even the most virtuous cause can be twisted into a tool of control. The strong mind does not allow itself to be led blindly, nor does it follow its own desires unquestioned. The only true defense against deception is wisdom, and wisdom is not found in certainty but in doubt tempered with reason.

Victory in war is not always marked by a conquered city or a fallen army. Sometimes, it is a nation led willingly to its own ruin, never knowing it was led at all. The greatest warriors of the mind do not fight battles; they shape them. And those who do not see the battlefield will find themselves unwittingly among the conquered.

Influence Campaigns

The battlefield has changed, but the nature of war remains the same. Where once armies marched and banners flew, now battles are waged in silence, unseen by those who are conquered. The ruler who understands this does not need to send soldiers to seize control of a nation; he need only guide the hands that mark the ballots, shape the minds that cast the votes, and ensure that his victory is written in the will of the people. Influence campaigns and cyber-enabled election interference are the new weapons of conquest, subtle yet devastating, for they do not break a nation's walls—they rot its foundation from within.

To control an election is not merely to manipulate the count of votes, for such a crude approach invites discovery and retaliation. The true strategist begins his work long before the first ballot is cast, shaping the perception of the people until they see his chosen outcome as their own desire. He does not tell them whom to trust; he makes them doubt all but his voice. He does not silence opposition; he ensures that it speaks in discord, so that even truth appears tainted by deceit. He does not destroy the system; he weakens faith in it, until even the victor stands upon uncertain ground.

The first strike in this battle is not with force but with whispers. The wise ruler spreads messages that divide, that inflame, that make allies turn upon one another. He does not need to create division where none exists; he need only widen the cracks already present. A society already fractured is a society easily led, for when the people war amongst themselves, they do not see the hand that guides their ruin. A campaign of influence is not merely the spread of propaganda—it is the careful planting of seeds, where every doubt, every fear, every long-standing grievance is nurtured into full bloom at the moment of decision.

But whispers alone do not win wars. The general who fights with information does not merely shape opinion; he bends reality itself. Through the tools of the digital age, he ensures that what the people see, what they read, what they believe is no longer their own choosing. He amplifies voices that serve his purpose, silences those that do not, and floods the field of discourse with so much noise that even the wise struggle to discern truth from illusion. The strength of cyber-enabled interference lies not in a single attack, but in the relentless erosion of certainty. A claim, repeated enough times, becomes indistinguishable from truth. A lie, buried in half-truths, becomes a foundation upon which entire movements stand.

To strike at the heart of a democracy, the attacker does not need to command armies; he need only control the flow of information. He does not need to change every mind; he need only sway enough. He does not need to forge a single vote; he need only create doubt in the legitimacy of the count. A nation whose people no longer trust its elections is a nation already defeated, for its own divisions will prevent it from standing strong against external threats. The enemy who weakens his foe without firing a shot is the most dangerous of all, for his victory is not one that can be undone by force—it is written in the minds of the conquered.

To defend against such an enemy requires more than vigilance; it requires wisdom. A people who understand the nature of deception will not be so easily deceived. A nation that values truth above convenience will not be so easily led astray. The ruler who seeks to protect his land must ensure that his people are not merely informed, but aware of the weapons used against them. He must guard not only the ballot box but the minds that determine its outcome. The greatest shield against manipulation is not censorship, nor counter-propaganda, but a citizenry that thinks, that questions, that sees the battle even when it is waged in shadows. Only then can a nation remain unconquered, not by force, but by the strength of its own wisdom.

Controlling the Narrative

The battle for power is not always fought on the field but in the minds of the people. To command an army is to control force, but to command belief is to control destiny. He who masters the narrative controls not only what the people think but how they think. A sword can silence a man, but a well-placed word can turn a thousand against him. The ruler who understands this does not rely on violence when persuasion can achieve greater ends. To control the narrative through media manipulation is to shape reality itself, for reality is not what is, but what is perceived.

The wise strategist knows that truth is pliable in the hands of the skilled. What is reported becomes what is believed; what is repeated becomes what is remembered. To shape the media is to shape the lens through which the people see the world. He who controls this lens does not need to fabricate falsehoods; he need only decide which truths to reveal and which to conceal. The story untold is as powerful as the story spoken. To control information is not merely to dictate what is said, but to ensure that what is unsaid is forgotten.

Victory in this war is not achieved by silencing all opposition, for silence breeds suspicion. The cunning ruler does not erase voices but drowns them. He allows his enemies to speak, but ensures that their words are lost in a flood of noise. He does not deny truth outright, for outright denial invites scrutiny. Instead, he offers many truths, conflicting and chaotic, so that certainty dissolves and confusion reigns. A confused people do not rise, for they cannot find solid ground upon which to stand.

To control the media is not simply to instruct it; it is to make it believe it acts of its own will. The most effective manipulation is that which is unseen, where the messengers believe themselves to be free even as they deliver the message of another. A ruler does not need to dictate every word if he controls the forces that shape discourse. He does not command what is written, but he ensures that the hands that write are rewarded for writing well. A journalist need not be coerced when he is led to believe that he has chosen his path willingly.

The skilled manipulator does not rely solely on the spoken word. Images, symbols, and the weight of silence itself all play their part in the orchestration of perception. The picture shown at the right moment, the emphasis placed on one event while another is ignored—these are the strokes of an artist painting a world that suits his design. He who wields the media does not need to tell the people what to think. He merely ensures that they never see an alternative.

The greatest threat to this strategy is a people who understand its nature. A mind aware of manipulation is a mind harder to control. The ruler who wishes to maintain his hold must ensure that skepticism itself is weaponized, turned inward so that distrust fractures rather than unites. He must make his critics doubt one another more than they doubt him. The strongest chains are those the prisoner defends, believing them to be his armor. If the people believe they are free even as they follow the path laid for them, then they are more bound than if they had been shackled openly.

To resist such control requires more than knowledge—it requires discipline. He who seeks truth must learn to separate signal from noise, to see not only what is shown but what is hidden. He must question not only the words spoken but the motives behind them. A people who wish to remain free must learn that their greatest weapon is not blind resistance, but clarity of thought. For in the war of the mind, he who sees through the fog of deception stands unconquered, no matter how great the force arrayed against him.

To wage war is to expend resources. The army that marches must be fed, the soldier that fights must be armed, and the kingdom that endures must be sustained. War has always been a contest of strength, but strength is not only measured in numbers or steel—it is measured in wealth, in the ability to project power without exhausting one's means. In the modern age, war has shifted from the battlefield to the network, from the sword to the algorithm, from the siege to the economic disruption of a nation's infrastructure. The economics of cyberwar is the art of achieving victory not through brute force, but by turning an enemy's own wealth and dependencies against him.

The wise general understands that traditional war is costly. The raising of armies, the forging of weapons, and the occupation of land all drain a nation's treasury. Even the victor suffers loss, for every battle fought demands tribute in gold and labor. But cyberwarfare offers a path where great damage can be inflicted at little cost. A single skilled warrior behind a screen may bring down systems that took millions to build. An empire that believes itself secure behind walls of steel may find its defenses crumbling with the press of a key. This is the power of cyberwar: to make the enemy spend without spending, to make him rebuild what has not been physically destroyed, to make him fight a battle that he cannot see.

To understand the economics of cyberwar is to understand that the greatest victories are those that make the enemy collapse under the weight of his own wealth. A nation that relies on technology is a nation vulnerable to its failure. The markets that drive economies are built on trust, and trust is a fragile thing. A rumor planted at the right moment can cause panic. A system disrupted at the right time can create financial ruin. An attack on infrastructure does not merely halt production; it causes a ripple that spreads, where uncertainty becomes fear, and fear becomes paralysis. He who can make the enemy's people lose faith in their own stability has already won half the war.

The strategist does not strike blindly. He knows that not all targets are equal, that not all wounds weaken the same. A nation may endure the loss of a battle, but can it endure the loss of its banking systems? Can it function without power, without water, without communication? Can it stand when its people no longer trust their currency, their transactions, their livelihoods? The true warrior of cyberwarfare does not seek destruction—he seeks disruption. He does not merely take from his enemy; he forces his enemy to spend, to waste, to collapse under the weight of his own necessary defense. A king who must constantly guard his treasury cannot focus on expansion, cannot invest in the future, cannot grow beyond the shadow of the war that drains him.

To fight such a war requires little in comparison to the cost it imposes. A sword must be forged, but a virus need only be written. A castle must be defended on all sides, but a network need only fail at one point. A single weakness, a single oversight, a single lapse in vigilance is all that is required for ruin. The attacker who understands this knows patience is his ally, for time is always in his favor. A strike today may cause an enemy to spend for years, not knowing if or when the next blow will come. The uncertainty itself is a weapon, for fear demands expenditure, and expenditure drains the will to fight.

A ruler who wishes to defend against such warfare must not only guard his wealth but understand that wealth itself can be turned against him. A nation too reliant on its systems without securing them is a fortress with open gates. A people who trust without question are a people already conquered. Defense is not merely in fortification but in adaptability, in the ability to shift, to recover, to build systems that do not crumble at the first sign of attack. The ruler who wishes to endure must make resilience his shield and vigilance his spear, for in cyberwar, it is not the strongest who survive, but the most prepared.

The war of the future is not fought with armies upon fields, but with economies that can be swayed, with infrastructures that can be broken, with wealth that can be stolen or rendered meaningless. The kingdom that does not recognize this truth will find itself defeated before it even knows a war has begun.

The Financial Impact

To wage war is to bleed, and in the age of cyberwarfare, blood is measured in coin. The greatest victories are won not by armies, but by draining the enemy of his wealth, forcing him to spend without end, weakening him until he is vulnerable to collapse. The financial impact of cyberattacks is not merely a sum to be counted—it is a weapon wielded against a nation's stability, its markets, its industries, and its people. The wise ruler does not only guard his borders; he guards his treasuries, for he who controls the flow of wealth controls the fate of empires.

The most effective strike is not always the most visible. A castle under siege knows its peril, but a kingdom whose wealth is slowly drained may not recognize its ruin until it is too late. A cyberattack does not need to destroy to be devastating; it need only disrupt. A single attack on financial institutions can send markets into chaos, as traders panic and wealth vanishes in moments. An attack on supply chains can halt production, raising costs, breaking trust, and making recovery more expensive than war itself. A well-placed breach into corporate systems can expose secrets, cripple negotiations, and turn a powerful enterprise into a house of sand.

The ruler who understands cyberwarfare does not seek only to steal, but to force his enemy to spend. A nation that must constantly defend itself from unseen threats is a nation forced to pour wealth into protection, into rebuilding, into the illusion of security. The attacker may expend little, crafting a simple but deadly intrusion, while the defender must spend vast fortunes to guard every possible weakness. It is a battle of patience, for the enemy who fights shadows will exhaust himself long before the one who strikes from them. A kingdom that cannot secure its wealth will find itself at the mercy of those who can take it without ever setting foot upon its land.

Commerce, the lifeblood of a nation, is vulnerable to manipulation. The destruction of a single banking system does not simply cause loss—it shatters confidence. If the people fear that their wealth is no longer safe, they will withdraw, they will hoard, they will cease to invest. When faith in the system is broken, the economy crumbles under its own weight. Trade slows, businesses fall, industries wither. The damage of a cyberattack does not end when the breach is sealed, for the wound festers long after, creating instability that the attacker may exploit at will. He who can make his enemy doubt his own foundations has already begun to bring them down.

The wise ruler does not wait for war to come; he prepares for it in times of peace. He does not merely react to attacks but fortifies his economy against their effects. A system built to withstand failure does not collapse when one part is struck. A people who trust in resilience do not succumb to fear when crisis arises. The defender who understands the cost of cyberwarfare does not spend recklessly but wisely, ensuring that his wealth is not merely a treasure to be taken, but a fortress that cannot be breached.

In the end, the true measure of a cyberattack is not in the money stolen, the systems breached, or the data lost, but in the ability of a nation to endure. The ruler who allows himself to be drawn into endless defense will find his wealth drained without his enemy ever raising a sword. But he who builds his economy to withstand the storms of war will find that no attack, no matter how precise, can bring him to ruin. To understand the financial impact of cyberattacks is to understand that war is no longer fought with armies alone, but with the invisible hands that shape the flow of wealth. And in this war, victory belongs not to the strongest, but to the most unshakable.

Digital Piracy

The art of war is not only fought with armies and weapons but with knowledge stolen in the shadows. A kingdom's strength is not merely in its walls but in the ideas that build them, the secrets that give it an edge over its rivals, the innovations that drive its people forward. To take these without battle is the mark of a superior strategist, for he who controls the flow of knowledge controls the battlefield itself. Digital piracy, intellectual property theft, and corporate espionage are the weapons of the unseen war, where victories are won not with force but with silence, and where the greatest conquests are those that go unnoticed.

To steal an idea is to deny its creator the fruits of his labor while enriching oneself without cost. The thief who takes knowledge need not forge, need not mine, need not toil—he need only extract and replicate. In the past, the theft of ideas required spies, bribery, and secrecy, but in the modern age, distance is no barrier, and the walls of even the mightiest citadel can be breached by a single unnoticed flaw in its digital defenses. The adversary who can reach into the vaults of another's mind and claim what is within does not need to fight for dominance; he has already acquired the means to surpass his foe.

A kingdom that fails to protect its creations will find itself laboring for the benefit of others. The merchant who invests in new designs, the inventor who forges new machines, the scholar who discovers new methods—all are powerless if their work is stolen before it can be secured. A nation that loses its intellectual wealth loses its future, for no matter how vast its resources, no matter how disciplined its people, it will always walk behind those who have taken what it should have protected. The ruler who does not guard his knowledge guards nothing at all, for a treasury emptied of gold can be refilled, but a treasury emptied of ideas leaves only stagnation and decay.

Corporate espionage is the weapon of those who seek power not through destruction but through the silent acquisition of advantage. The strongest company is not the one with the greatest wealth, but the one that possesses the most valuable knowledge, the plans that shape the future, the innovations that others have yet to imagine. To infiltrate a rival's secrets is to deny him his edge, to walk his path before he himself can tread it. The warrior who fights with swords risks loss, but the warrior who fights with stolen knowledge ensures that his enemy's strength becomes his own. The corporation that falls victim to espionage does not realize it has been defeated until the moment its rival unveils what it thought was uniquely its own.

The battlefield of the digital world is one where the thief has the advantage, for he needs only to succeed once, while the defender must be vigilant always. The ruler who seeks to protect his kingdom's mind must understand that walls built of data are more fragile than walls built of stone. He must not only guard against intrusion but ensure that even what is stolen is of little use. The wise general does not merely build strong defenses; he builds defenses that mislead, that entrap, that make the thief believe he has taken something valuable when in truth he has taken only that which was meant for him to find. A kingdom that understands this turns theft into a weapon, making the adversary waste time, effort, and resources chasing shadows.

A people who value knowledge must treat it as they would their greatest treasure, for in the age of information, what is most valuable is not gold, nor land, nor even armies—it is the secrets that allow a kingdom to rise. To fail to protect them is to leave the gates open to conquest. The true master of war does not seek to take by force what he can acquire without battle, and the wise ruler does not wait to be plundered before fortifying his greatest wealth. The war of the future is fought not over territory, but over thought, and he who does not see this war will find himself conquered before he even knows it has begun.

Cryptocurrency

The battlefield of war is no longer bound by land, sea, or air; it is fought in the unseen currents of the digital world, where wealth moves without borders and transactions leave no footprints. The ruler who understands this does not seek to fund his operations through traditional means, for the treasury of old is slow, traceable, and vulnerable. He who masters the art of cyber warfare knows that power is no longer held in vaults but in codes, and that cryptocurrency is the river that feeds the armies of the unseen war. To control this river is to control the flow of war itself.

Gold weighs down an army, but cryptocurrency moves like the wind. The strategist who wishes to fund his warriors in the digital realm does not need to transport coin, does not need to move wealth through the hands of men who may betray him. He simply disperses it across the blockchain, where it is shielded from prying eyes, where it can be sent with the swiftness of thought itself. The traditional treasuries of nations are bound by law, by oversight, by the careful watch of those who seek to control the flow of wealth. But the digital currency is free from these chains, operating beyond the reach of kings and their accountants. It is the perfect tool for those who wish to fund war without revealing their hand.

A wise general does not fight a war that he cannot afford. He does not arm his soldiers only to be weakened by the cost of his own strength. Cryptocurrency allows him to fund his forces without constraint, to pay mercenaries without allegiance, to move his wealth without being hindered by the enemy's watchful gaze. He who understands this will not rely on traditional systems, where transactions can be frozen, where accounts can be seized, where gold can be traced back to its source. Instead, he will ensure that his operations are fueled by a currency that cannot be touched, that cannot be stopped, that cannot be controlled by those who would seek to cut off his supply.

The greatest advantage of cryptocurrency in cyber operations is not only its secrecy but its ability to empower warriors who fight in the shadows. A lone hacker, armed with nothing but his knowledge, can be paid as easily as an army, and his skills may be worth more than legions. The strategist who wishes to cripple his enemy does not need to build war machines; he needs only to fund those who can infiltrate, disrupt, and dismantle. The cyber warrior who receives payment in cryptocurrency does not wait for approval, does not rely on banks, does not fear sanctions. He acts as soon as his reward is delivered, striking before his target even knows he has been seen.

The ruler who fails to recognize the power of this new form of wealth will find himself blind to the movements of his enemies. He will look for supply lines that do not exist, for meetings that never happen, for trails of gold that were never laid. The war funded by cryptocurrency is a war that cannot be starved, for the enemy who fights with such a treasury does not need to smuggle weapons across borders or find allies willing to take risks. He moves unseen, his soldiers appearing from nowhere, his influence spreading without the need for physical presence. He is as the wind, touching all but grasped by none.

To fight this war, a ruler must understand that the battlefield has changed. He must not only guard against traditional threats but must learn to see the invisible streams of wealth that fuel his enemies. The defender who does not prepare for this war will find that he is already defeated, for his enemy has been armed and paid long before he even knew the battle had begun. To understand the role of cryptocurrency in cyber operations is to understand that the wars of the future will not be fought with swords, nor with bullets, nor even with soldiers—but with wealth that cannot be seized, warriors who cannot be traced, and conflicts that do not announce themselves until the moment of their victory.

The wise ruler knows that war is not a thing of the past, nor is it bound by the weapons of old. The battlefield shifts, the warriors change, but the struggle for dominance remains eternal. He who prepares for yesterday's war is already defeated, while he who looks ahead shapes the course of battle before the first strike is made. The future of cyberwarfare is not written in steel or fire, but in data, in control, in the mastery of unseen forces that shape the world. To understand this future is to wield power before one's enemies even comprehend its existence.

The nature of war is to control, to impose one's will upon another. In the past, this was done through conquest of land, through the destruction of cities, through the breaking of armies. In the age of cyberwarfare, victory is achieved without banners, without open battle, without the conquered ever realizing they have been subdued. He who masters the digital realm does not need to invade a nation to rule it; he need only control its systems, its networks, the flow of its information. A nation that cannot command its own technology is already a vassal to those who can.

The wars of the future will not be fought with single strikes, but with persistent campaigns of influence and disruption. The enemy will not always know he is under attack. His people will not see invaders marching upon his cities, yet their world will begin to shift, their faith in their own institutions will waver, their leaders will act as if they are free while unknowingly dancing to the strings of another. The ruler who understands this will not seek to merely break his enemy's defenses; he will ensure that his enemy does not even recognize where the battlefield lies.

A kingdom's strength no longer rests solely in its armies, nor in its economy, but in its ability to protect and control its digital sovereignty. The strongest walls mean nothing if the gates of data are left open, if the knowledge of its people, the movements of its wealth, the pulse of its industries are all visible to an enemy who does not show his face. He who can predict the actions of a nation before they are taken has already won half the war. He who can alter them without the nation knowing has won it entirely.

The weapons of cyberwarfare will grow more subtle, more intelligent, more autonomous. Attacks will not be conducted merely by soldiers at keyboards, but by algorithms that learn, that adapt, that strike without needing direction. The enemy of tomorrow may not even be a man but a system, one that infiltrates, disrupts, and dismantles without emotion, without hesitation, without error. A nation that does not prepare for this will find itself overwhelmed, not by a mighty army, but by countless, invisible blades that carve away its strength piece by piece.

The wise ruler will ensure that his people do not become complacent, that they do not mistake peace for security, that they understand war is no longer declared—it is simply waged. He will train his forces not merely in defense, but in resilience, in deception, in the ability to turn an attack back upon its source. The best defense is not an unbreachable fortress but the ability to rebuild faster than the enemy can destroy, to make attacks costly, to ensure that any who strike will pay a price they cannot afford.

To control the future of war is to control the tools upon which all nations now rely. The ruler who allows his enemies to command his networks, his satellites, his artificial minds will find himself a king in name only, his people subjects to a power they cannot see. The future of cyberwarfare is the future of war itself, and he who does not prepare for it has already surrendered.

AI and Quantum Computing

The nature of war evolves as the weapons of battle change. The ruler who clings to the tools of the past will find himself defenseless before enemies who wield the future. The mind that understands war does not only study the conflicts of today but looks beyond, seeking to master the forces that will shape tomorrow. In the coming age, power will not belong to those who wield the strongest armies, nor to those who control the greatest wealth, but to those who command the forces of artificial intelligence and quantum computing. These are not merely tools; they are the architects of a new battlefield, one where the victor will be he who bends reality to his will before his enemy even sees the battle begin.

Artificial intelligence is both sword and shield, capable of defending a kingdom or destroying it from within. The general who controls AI does not need legions of men when he can command legions of machines, entities that do not tire, do not question, do not fail. A well-trained army of AI systems can identify weaknesses before an enemy knows they exist, strike at vulnerabilities before they can be fortified, and disrupt entire networks without a single soldier stepping onto the battlefield. The greatest power of AI is not in brute force but in the ability to shape perception, to guide decisions, to create illusions so complete that an enemy acts against his own interests without realizing he has been deceived.

The warrior who wields AI does not merely attack; he learns. Every failed strike is a lesson, every defense encountered is a blueprint for its undoing. The enemy who believes he has found safety will soon find that his movements have been predicted, his countermeasures rendered useless before he deploys them. No fortress is secure when its defenses have already been mapped, no army is powerful when its strategies have already been countered. The ruler who seeks victory in this new age must not only command his warriors but command the intelligence that guides them, for war will no longer be won by strength alone, but by the mind that can outthink even the fastest machine.

Yet even as AI reshapes the battlefield, a greater force looms on the horizon, one that will unravel the very foundations of modern security. Quantum computing is not merely a weapon; it is a force that alters the nature of war itself. The encryption that shields nations, that protects secrets, that secures the flow of wealth and information—this will crumble before the might of quantum codebreakers. The ruler who first masters this power will see his enemies laid bare before him, their most guarded secrets exposed as if they had been shouted in the open. He will strike with knowledge that cannot be concealed, and his enemies will find themselves naked before his gaze.

The wise general knows that the greatest power is not to attack but to make an attack unnecessary. He who commands quantum computing will not need to breach defenses; he will simply render them irrelevant. His enemies will scramble to defend what has already been taken, will waste their strength securing doors that have already been opened. The ruler who does not prepare for this shift will find his kingdom vulnerable not to an invading army but to an enemy who already knows his every move before it is made.

To survive the wars of the future, one must not merely react to threats but anticipate them. He who builds his defenses for today's war will be undone by tomorrow's weapons. The kingdom that hopes to endure must prepare now for a battlefield that does not yet exist, for the enemy who does not yet march, for the weapons that have not yet been revealed. In the coming war, victory will not belong to the strongest, nor to the richest, but to the one who commands the unseen, who shapes the future before his enemies can grasp it. To control AI and quantum computing is to control war itself, and he who masters them first will hold power beyond the reach of all who come after.

Ethical Dilemmas

The greatest victories are not always won with steel and fire but with decisions that shape the battlefield before the first strike is made. In the age of autonomous digital warfare, the general no longer commands men alone but machines that act without hesitation, without doubt, without fear. The wise ruler must ask whether power without conscience is strength or folly, for a weapon that cannot question its purpose may one day turn upon those who wield it. The greatest challenge of this new war is not in its execution but in its restraint, in the choices made before the first machine is set upon its path.

To entrust war to machines is to surrender control over life and death to something that does not know the value of either. The warrior who fights with his hands understands the weight of his actions, but the machine, given a task, executes without reflection. The strategist who unleashes autonomous forces upon the world must recognize that he has created something that cannot know mercy, that does not distinguish between victory and ruin. A sword in the hands of a man may be restrained, but a sword with no hand to hold it knows only its edge.

The ruler who embraces autonomous digital warfare must understand the balance between efficiency and destruction. To remove the soldier from the battlefield is to spare him from death, but it is also to remove the final barrier between war and annihilation. A human soldier hesitates, questions, weighs the morality of his actions. A machine does not. The general who replaces his warriors with algorithms may find that he has created a force that obeys too well, that carries out his will even when his will changes. He who commands such a force must ensure that his commands are wise, for once set in motion, such war does not slow, does not reconsider, does not turn back.

The battlefield no longer belongs to those who march but to those who code. The strategist of the future will not only design tactics but the very nature of the warrior itself. The dilemma is not only in who fights but in who decides. If war is fought by machines, then who bears the burden of responsibility? If an autonomous force commits destruction beyond what was intended, who answers for its actions? The ruler who believes he can avoid accountability by blaming his creation is a fool, for war does not absolve those who unleash it. The enemy will not negotiate with a machine, nor will the people forgive a ruler who cannot explain the actions of his own forces.

The greatest danger in autonomous warfare is not only in what is done but in what is lost. A war fought by men teaches the cost of battle, the weight of loss, the importance of restraint. A war fought by machines risks becoming endless, for without the sacrifice of blood, there is little to slow its advance. The ruler who does not feel the suffering of his people may send his machines to fight without pause, believing that victory is inevitable. But war without cost is war without limit, and the battlefield of tomorrow may stretch beyond what any ruler can control. To wield such power without wisdom is to invite disaster, for once the sword is drawn, it does not easily return to its sheath.

The wise ruler does not reject progress, nor does he fear technology, but he understands that every weapon demands discipline. The strongest warrior is not the one who strikes hardest, but the one who knows when not to strike at all. To use autonomous warfare is to walk a path from which there is no return, for a world that fights with machines will not again fight without them. The decision is not whether this future will come, for it already approaches. The decision is whether those who guide it will do so with wisdom, with restraint, and with an understanding that power without judgment is not strength, but the beginning of ruin.

Cyber Treaties

The wise ruler knows that war without rules is destruction without end. In the battles of old, warriors fought with honor, with codes that bound even the fiercest enemies to certain limits. But in the age of cyberwarfare, the battlefield has no borders, no laws, no certainty. A strike may come from nowhere and leave no trace of its origin. A kingdom may fall without ever seeing the face of its conqueror. Without agreements to govern this new war, chaos reigns, and he who strikes first rules the battlefield, while those who seek peace find themselves defenseless.

To fight without rules is to invite ruin, not only for the enemy but for oneself. The general who believes he can wield cyberwarfare as a weapon without consequence will one day find his own gates broken by the very same methods he once used. No fortress is impenetrable, no system unbreakable, no nation beyond the reach of digital war. He who believes himself safe in this new age is already vulnerable, for every kingdom now relies upon the networks that sustain it. A strike against one may ripple outward, breaking more than the target, collapsing entire systems that sustain economies, governments, and the lives of those who do not even know they are at war.

The greatest threat is not the enemy one sees but the one who strikes from the shadows, unbound by consequence. In war fought with steel, a soldier knows his adversary. He sees the banners of his foe, the army that marches against him. But in the world of cyberwarfare, there are no banners, only silence before devastation. Without clear rules of engagement, there can be no certainty, no stability, only the endless fear of unseen enemies waiting to strike. He who understands this knows that war cannot be allowed to descend into endless uncertainty, for a world without rules is a world where all are vulnerable, where no power remains safe.

To craft treaties is not to show weakness but to ensure that war does not consume all who wage it. The strongest ruler is not the one who destroys his enemies without limit, but the one who secures peace without surrendering his strength. Agreements among nations do not prevent war but ensure that when war comes, it does not bring ruin to all. Even the mightiest empires of old understood that war must be bound by limits, that certain lines must never be crossed, lest the battle destroy not only the enemy but the victor as well. The same must be true in the digital age, where the weapons of war do not leave bodies on battlefields but shatter economies, cripple infrastructure, and leave the world more fragile with every silent attack.

The wise general understands that a battle fought with restraint is one that can be won. He does not seek total destruction, for total destruction leaves nothing to rule. A ruler who believes he can unleash cyberwarfare without consequence will soon learn that his own kingdom stands upon the same fragile ground. The networks he relies upon are not invulnerable, the systems he commands are not unbreakable, and the moment his enemies have nothing left to lose, they will strike without fear, for there will be no rules left to restrain them. He who burns the bridges of diplomacy will find himself isolated when the fires he started turn upon his own land.

To establish global cyber treaties is not to deny war, but to shape it before it spirals beyond control. The strategist who sees the future knows that an ungoverned battlefield benefits no one, that war without limits ensures mutual destruction. Those who believe they can win without consequence must look beyond their own moment of advantage, for in time, the tide of war shifts, and those who once ruled the digital battlefield will find themselves besieged by forces they can no longer contain. The strongest nations are those that understand not only how to wield power but how to protect themselves from the reckless use of it.

The war of the future will not be fought with borders, nor will it be won with brute force alone. It will be shaped by those who control the rules, by those who understand that even in conflict, there must be order. The ruler who sees this truth will seek not endless war but a battlefield that does not lead to his own destruction. In the end, treaties are not made for the weak but for those who understand that strength is not only in conquest but in survival. He who builds the framework of war before it begins ensures that he is not consumed by it when it arrives.

Chapter 12 The Nature of Warfare

War does not end. It only changes its form, adapting
to the weapons and the minds that wield them. The
ruler who believes that the age of the sword has
passed is a fool, for the struggle for dominance, the
contest of wills, and the pursuit of victory remain
eternal. The battlefield has shifted from the fields of
blood to the realm of code, from the clash of steel to
the silent war of data and deception. Yet the essence
of war is unchanged, for it is not fought with weapons
alone but with strategy, patience, and the will to
outmaneuver the enemy. The enduring nature of
warfare in the cyber age is a truth that cannot be
ignored, for he who does not prepare for war will find
himself its first victim.

To control the enemy is to control his perception. In
the wars of old, armies marched upon the land,
banners high, their strength made visible for all to
see. In the war of the cyber age, the enemy does not
always know he is under attack. His systems are
infiltrated, his networks compromised, his people
misled, and yet he continues as if all is well, unaware
that his kingdom is crumbling beneath him. He who
understands this does not need to fire a shot, does not
need to breach a wall, for he can make the enemy

collapse under the weight of his own ignorance. To shape the battlefield without revealing the battle is the mark of a true strategist, and in the digital world, the unseen war is the most dangerous of all.

The warrior of this new age does not rely on brute force but on mastery of the unseen. His weapons are not swords but algorithms, not catapults but lines of code that dismantle defenses without making a sound. Yet the principles remain unchanged, for victory still belongs to the one who knows his enemy better than the enemy knows himself. The one who acts before the battle begins, who prepares while others remain blind, who strikes at the mind before striking at the body—he is the one who will claim victory. In the cyber age, as in all ages, the battle is won long before the enemy understands that he is fighting.

No fortress is impenetrable, no defense absolute. The greatest walls in history have fallen, and so too will the greatest systems of security be breached. The mistake of the overconfident ruler is to believe that he is untouchable, that his kingdom is secure, that his enemies lack the skill or the will to challenge him. Yet all systems are created by men, and all men make errors. A single flaw, a single moment of negligence, is enough for an adversary to slip through. He who does not seek out his own weaknesses before his enemy does is already lost. To endure in war is not to believe in invincibility but to understand that vigilance must never cease.

Time changes all things, but it does not change the heart of war. The tools of battle may evolve, but the nature of conflict remains constant. It is a contest of deception, of resourcefulness, of the ability to impose one's will upon another. The general who triumphs in the digital age does not do so because of superior technology alone, but because he understands the eternal truths of warfare. He knows that the enemy's strength can be turned against him, that fear is more powerful than any weapon, that the mind is the first battlefield upon which victory is decided. The strategist who embraces these truths will command not only his armies but the very shape of the conflict itself.

To believe that the cyber age has changed war is to misunderstand war entirely. The form shifts, but the struggle remains. The wise ruler does not focus only on new weapons but on timeless strategy, for he knows that war is as it has always been: the contest of those who see and those who are blind, of those who strike first and those who react too late, of those who command the battle before their enemy even knows it has begun. He who understands that war never truly ends will never be unprepared. He will not fear the battles to come, for he has already won them in the silence before the storm.

Applying Sun Tzu's Principles to Modern Conflicts

War is eternal, though its form is ever-changing. The wise general understands that the principles of victory do not shift with time, only the tools by which war is waged. The armies of the past rode on horseback; those of today move with machines and data, yet the contest remains the same: to subdue the enemy before battle begins, to control without force, to shape the field so that victory is assured before the first strike is made. He who applies the wisdom of the ancients to the conflicts of today does not seek merely to match his enemy in power but to outthink him, to win not through destruction but through mastery of the unseen forces that shape war.

To engage in direct conflict is to risk the unknown. The greatest victory is to make the enemy yield without battle, to cause him to see his own defeat before he even considers war. In modern conflict, the battlefield is not only the land, sea, and air but the mind, the network, the very perception of reality itself. The ruler who understands this does not rely solely on weapons of steel, for he knows that war begins long before the armies assemble. The enemy who believes he has already lost is the easiest to conquer. The enemy who doubts his own strength will surrender it willingly. War in the modern age is fought in whispers, in narratives, in unseen pressures that break the will before a single shot is fired.

To control information is to control war itself. The victorious ruler does not fight armies; he fights ideas, shaping the battlefield so that his enemy moves as he wills, believes as he wishes, and acts as he predicts. The soldier who enters the battlefield with a clouded mind is already lost, for confusion breeds hesitation, and hesitation leads to ruin. In modern conflict, perception is as powerful as any weapon. A nation may be strong in force yet weak in will, and he who shapes the perception of strength or weakness wields a weapon greater than any sword. The wise general understands that truth itself is a tool, that what the enemy believes determines his actions. A battlefield properly shaped ensures that war ends before it begins.

The direct assault is the path of last resort. He who rushes to battle without preparation is like the river that crashes against stone, exhausting itself without making progress. The victorious general flows like water, finding the enemy's weakness, pressing only where resistance is absent, reshaping the field so that the enemy's own strength becomes his downfall. In modern conflict, this means striking not at the enemy's might, but at his foundation. A nation does not fall when its army is defeated; it falls when its people no longer believe in its cause. The strongest weapon is not the missile, nor the soldier, nor the machine, but the doubt planted deep, the fear that spreads unseen, the certainty that crumbles from within.

To master modern warfare is to understand that it is not a contest of weapons but of time, patience, and perception. The general who rushes to fight exhausts himself; the general who waits and maneuvers wins before battle is necessary. He who commands war in the modern age does not think in battles but in years, does not seek to defeat his enemy but to make his enemy defeat himself. The war of today is not won in a single engagement but in the slow turning of forces, in the gradual weakening of resolve, in the battle that is fought not in the open but in the unseen struggles of influence, control, and deception.

The principles of Sun Tzu remain as unbreakable as the laws of nature. War is won not by force but by understanding, not by destruction but by shaping the battlefield before the first move is made. The ruler who knows this does not fear his enemy, for he has already made the enemy fear himself. Victory belongs not to the strongest, nor to the most aggressive, but to the one who sees the field most clearly, who moves with precision, who ensures that the battle is already decided before the enemy even knows he is at war.

Responsibility

War is not waged by armies alone, nor is defense the duty of a single ruler. In the age of cyberwarfare, the battlefield is everywhere, and those who fail to recognize their place in it are already defeated. The wise ruler understands that the strength of a kingdom is not held only in its soldiers but in the vigilance of its people, in the resilience of its structures, in the wisdom of its leaders. The responsibility of nations, corporations, and individuals in cyber defense is not a question of choice but of survival. He who neglects his role invites ruin, for an undefended gate is an invitation to conquest, and in the digital world, every gate is a potential breach.

The ruler who believes that cyber defense is the burden of warriors alone will find his kingdom vulnerable where he least expects it. A nation is not defended solely by firewalls and encryption, but by the discipline of its people, by the strength of its institutions, by the unity of those who stand to lose everything if they do not stand together. The enemy does not always strike with force; he strikes with deception, with silence, with the turning of allies into threats and trust into weakness. A kingdom that does not train its people to recognize these threats has already surrendered its security, for the greatest vulnerability is the mind that believes it is safe when it is not.

A corporation that values only profit and ignores the duty of defense builds its wealth upon shifting sands. The general who neglects his supply lines will soon find his army starving, and so too will the company that ignores cyber defense find itself at the mercy of those who take without effort. The trader who does not secure his transactions will find his wealth stolen. The builder who does not protect his designs will see them claimed by another. The merchant who does not safeguard his customers will find them turned against him when their trust is broken. He who understands that cyber defense is not merely protection but the foundation of stability will ensure that his strength is not easily taken.

An individual who believes himself too small to matter is already conquered. The soldier who does not sharpen his sword, believing that others will fight in his place, will be the first to fall. The citizen who ignores the threat before him, believing that defense is the duty of others, is the weakness through which the enemy will strike. The enemy does not need to breach walls if he can walk through open doors. The warrior who leaves his weapon unguarded gives his enemy the means to destroy him. The citizen who does not question what he sees, who does not defend his own mind, is as useful to the enemy as a traitor within the gates.

To defend against the threats of the digital age, all must recognize their role in the battle. A nation that prepares its people to see the war before it begins will not be caught unaware. A corporation that builds its wealth upon security will not crumble when the storm comes. An individual who understands that knowledge is the first line of defense will not be so easily deceived. The ruler who ensures that all are vigilant, that all understand their duty, that all recognize the war before it reaches their doorstep, is the ruler whose kingdom will endure.

The greatest defense is not an unbreakable wall but an unbreakable will. He who prepares before the attack does not fear the enemy, for he has already closed the doors through which the enemy would enter. The responsibility of cyber defense is not for the few but for all, for in war, it is not only the warrior who falls when the battle is lost, but the kingdom itself. The wise do not wait for war to teach them this truth; they act before the enemy moves, ensuring that when the storm comes, it breaks against a fortress that cannot fall.